DUBLIN

STREET & ATLAS GUIDE

CONTENTS

Scale of maps is 1:15,000 (4.2 inches to 1 mile)

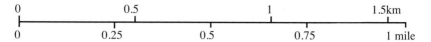

LEGEND

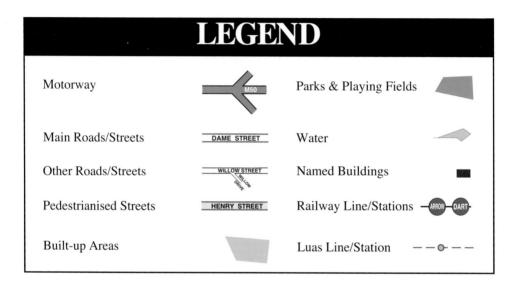

© Causeway Press (N.I.)

The maps on pages 4 to 41 are based on Ordnance Survey Ireland by permission of the Government. © Government of Ireland Permit Number 8423

Printed in Ireland by Graham & Heslip Ltd.

Edited by Paul Slevin. Comments, suggestions and inquiries should be addressed to him at the address below. Published by Causeway Press (N.I.), 17 Osborne Park, Bangor, N.Ireland BT20 3DJ. Phone UK 07768 172442. E-mail paulslevin@talk21.com

DISTRIBUTION: Distributed by Eason Wholesale Books (Phone Dublin 844 8888) and Argosy Libraries Ltd (Phone Dublin 823 9500). Quote ISBN 978 1 872600 44 4

ACKNOWLEDGMENTS: Thanks go to Catherine Coyle, Jo Turner, Ron Turner, Margaret Coyle and Michael Moriarty for their contributions.

DUBLIN
STREET ATLAS & GUIDE

We all like to kill two birds with one stone, so to speak, but the Dublin Street Atlas & Guide is that extremely rare bird which offers several different products for the price of one.

Firstly, it is a street atlas of the Dublin area, based on the latest Ordnance Survey. These maps, together with separate rail and bus maps, will help you to navigate your way through and around the city.

Secondly, it is a detailed guide to the best of what Dublin has to offer. Whether you are visiting for the first time or have lived here all your life, our aim is to help you make the most of this vibrant and colourful city.

The guide is written and published in Ireland, and is based on contributions from people who have immersed themselves in the Dublin social scene with scant regard to their need of sleep or the health of their livers. Having said that, we are always keen to hear alternative views. If you have any recommendations to make or any contrary views to express regarding any of our choices, please write, or e-mail to the addresses given on the page opposite. Any contributions which we use in the future will be acknowledged and a copy of the next edition will be sent in return for the best letters.

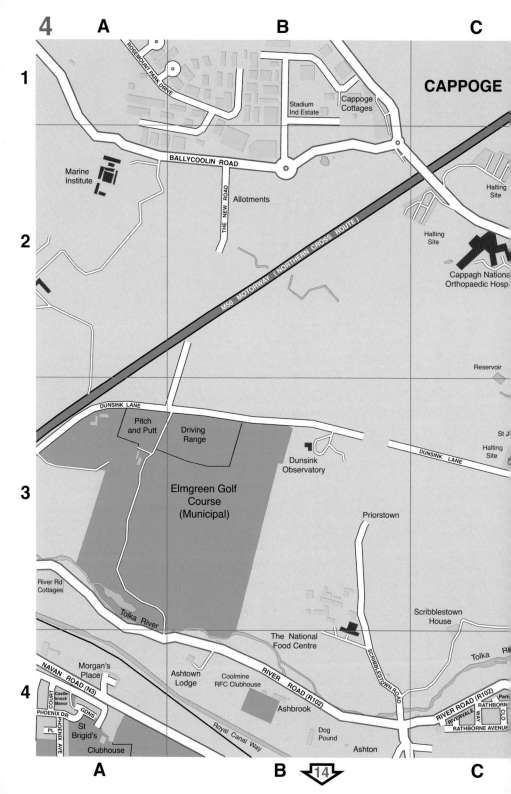

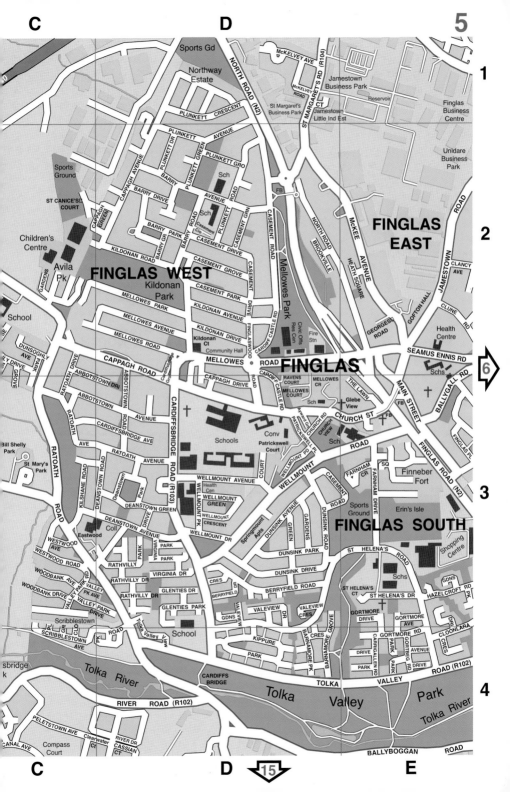

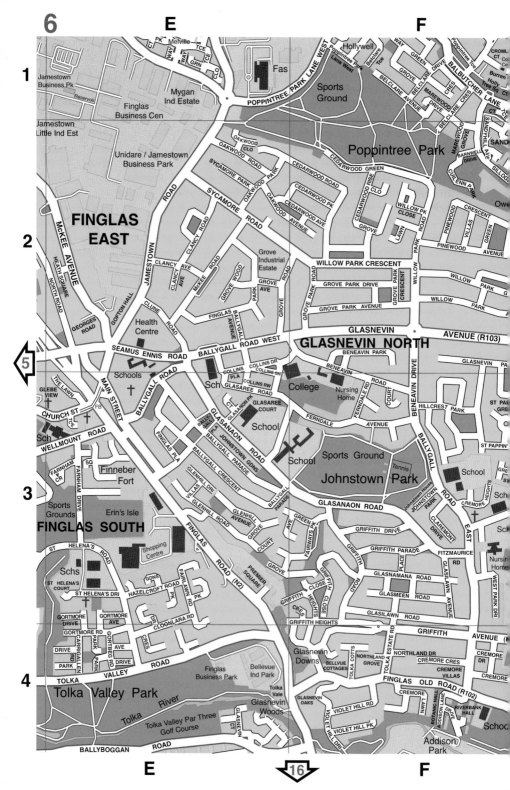

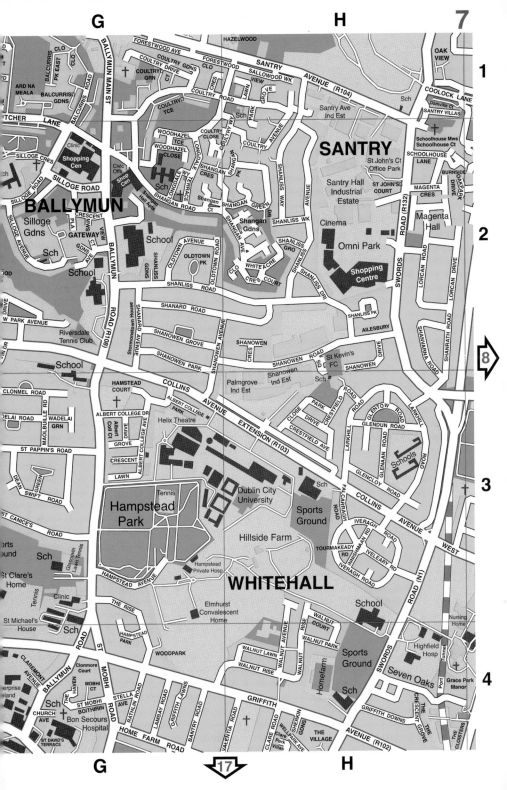

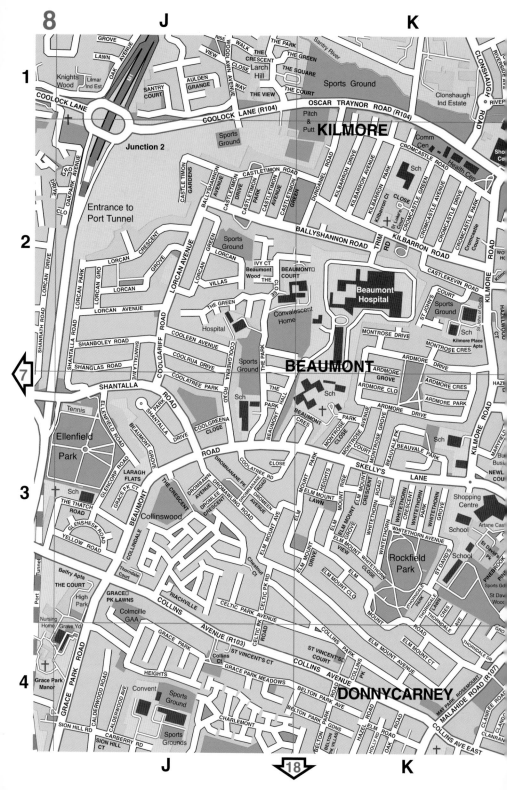

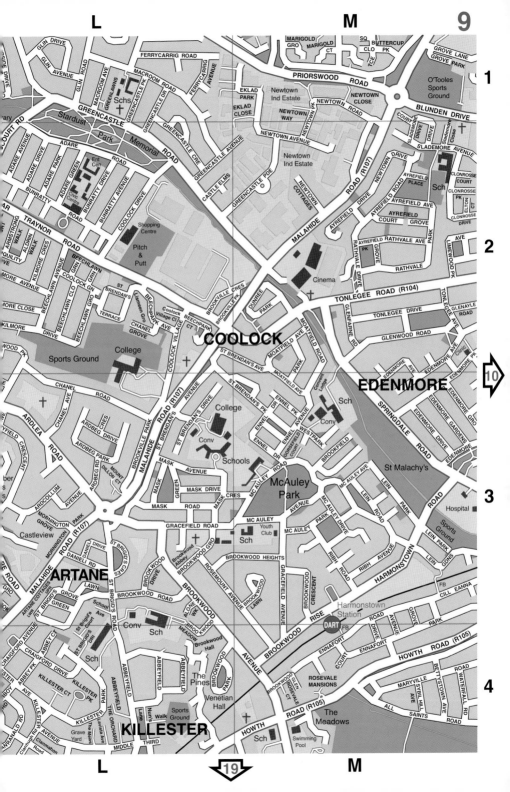

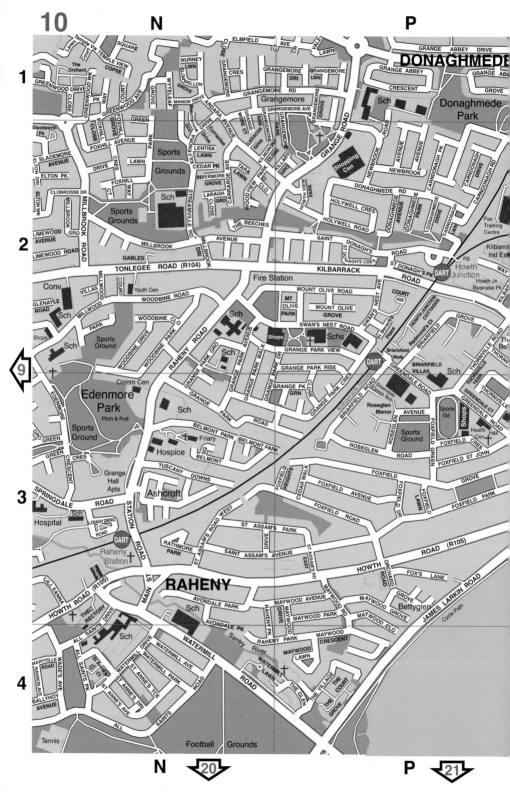

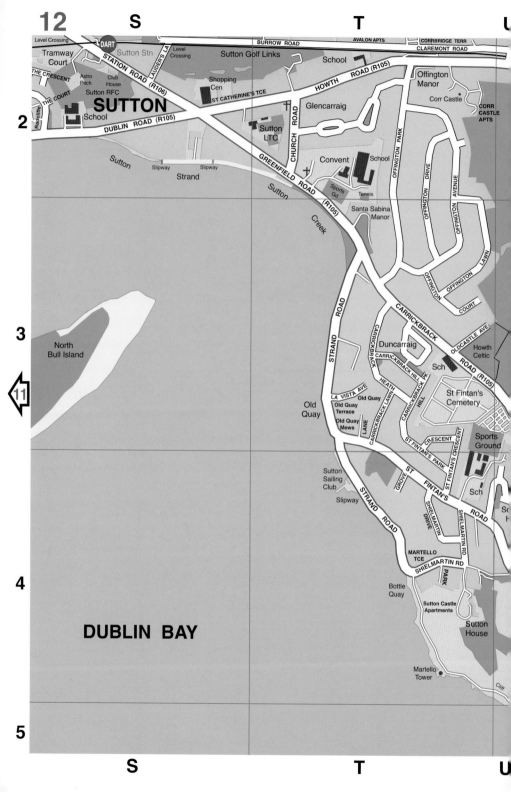

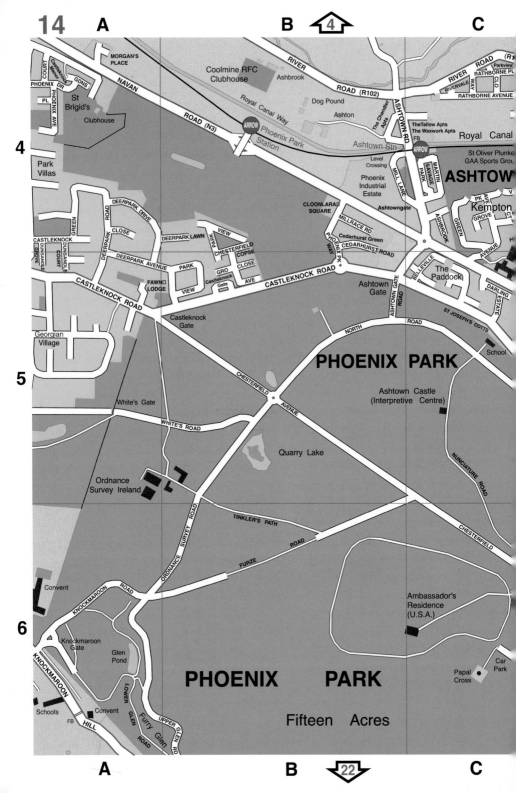

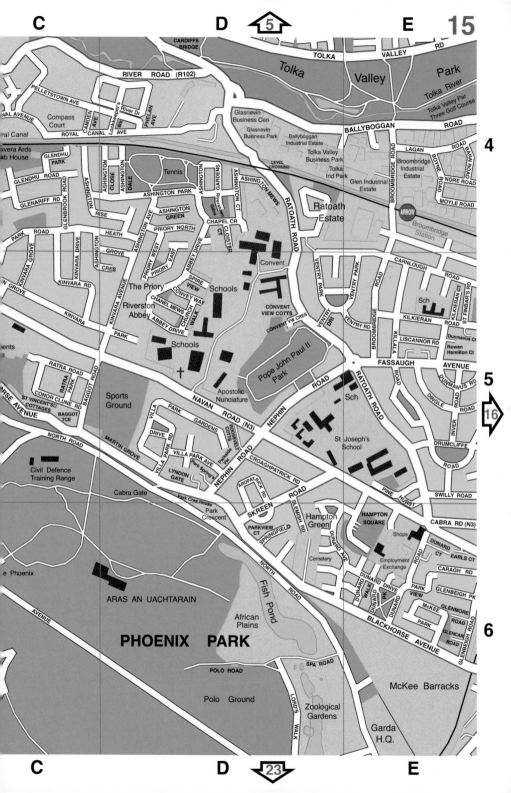

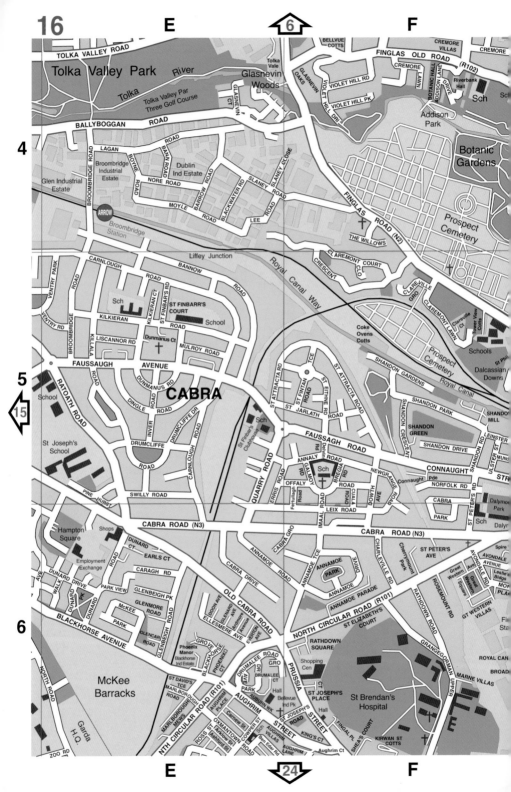

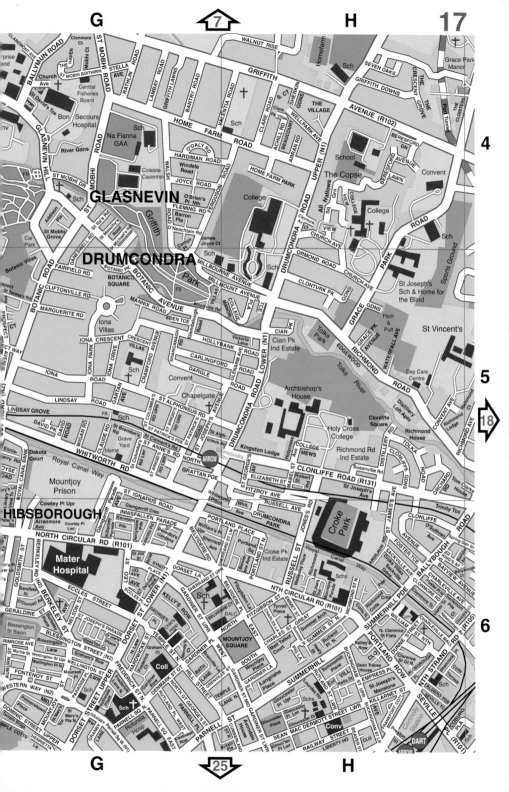

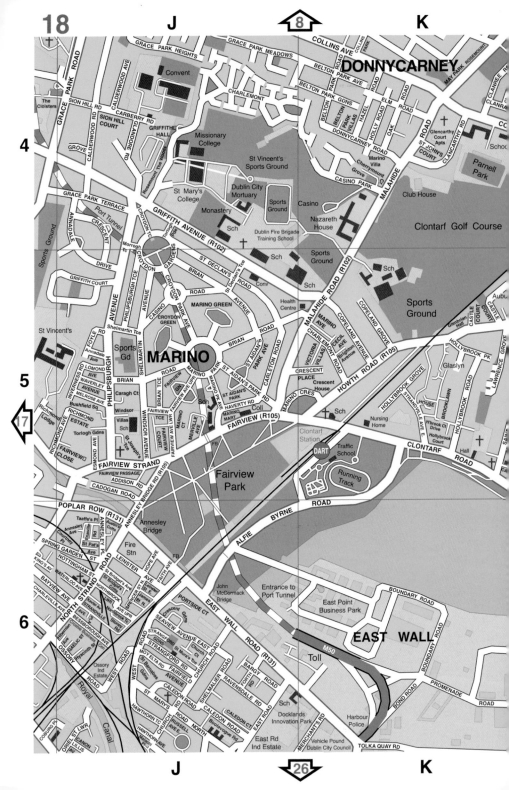

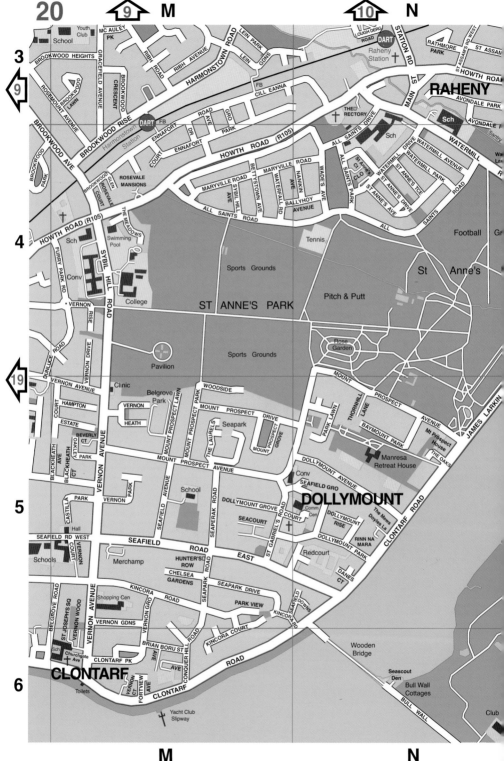

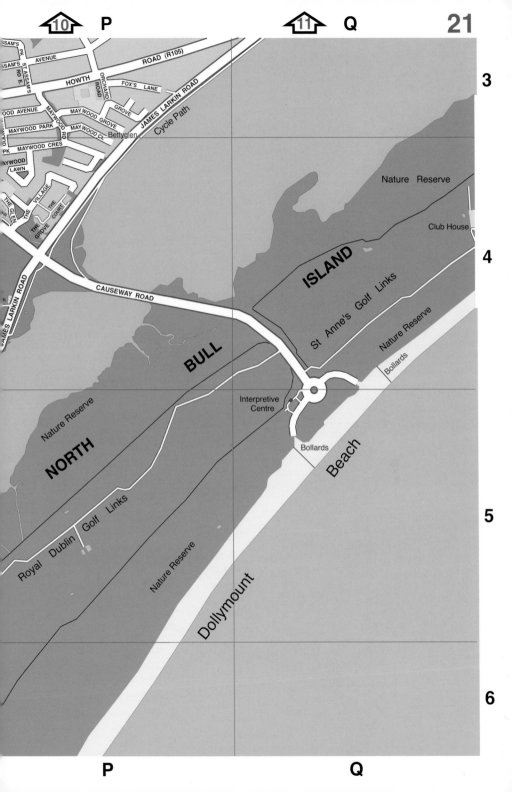

3

4

5

6

SSAM'S PK
SSAM'S ST ASSAM'S
RD E.
ST ASSAM'S
AVENUE
ROAD (R105)
HOWTH
ORCHARD ROAD
FOX'S LANE
JAMES LARKIN ROAD
Cycle Path
OOD AVENUE
MAYWOOD GROVE
GROVE
MAYWOOD RD
MAYWOOD PARK
MAYWOOD CL
Bettyglen
MAYWOOD CRES
PK
AYWOOD
LAWN
THE GLEN
THE GROVE
THE VILLAGE
THE COURT

JAMES LARKIN ROAD

CAUSEWAY ROAD

Nature Reserve

Club House

ISLAND

St Anne's Golf Links

Nature Reserve

Bollards

BULL

Nature Reserve

Interpretive Centre

Bollards

Beach

NORTH

Royal Dublin Golf Links

Nature Reserve

Dollymount

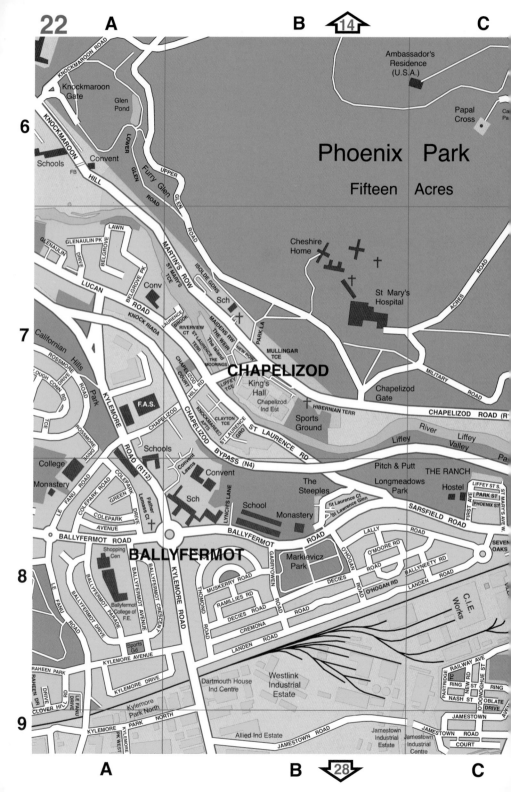

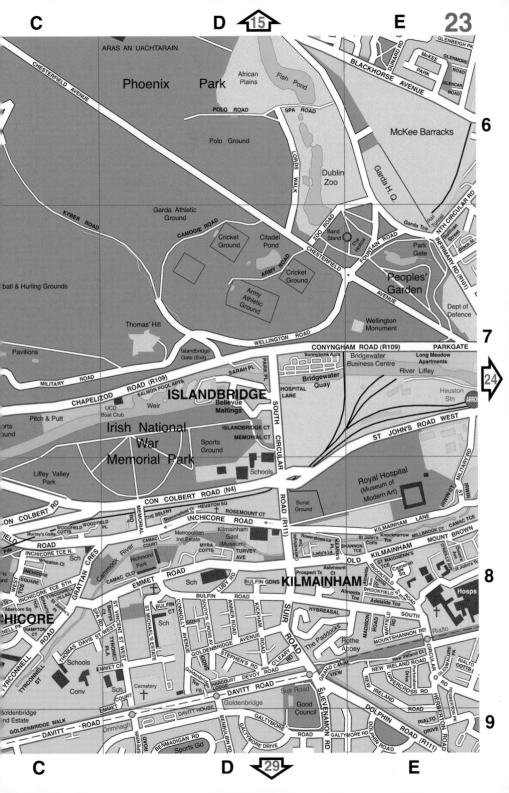

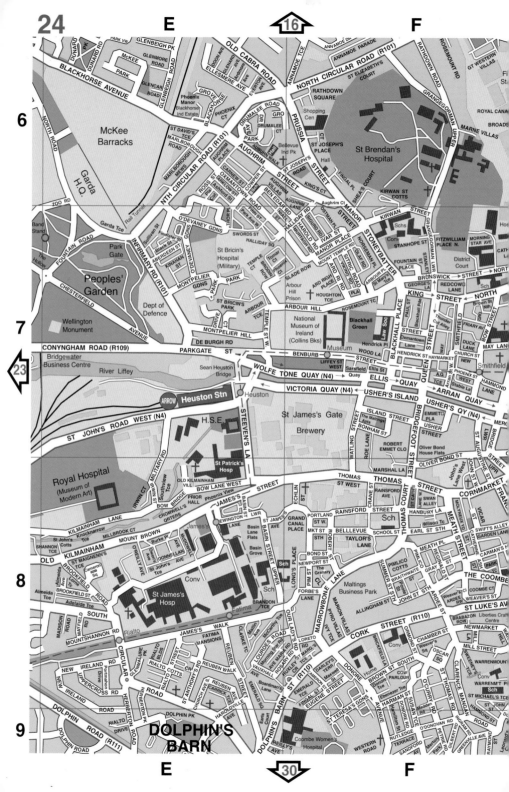

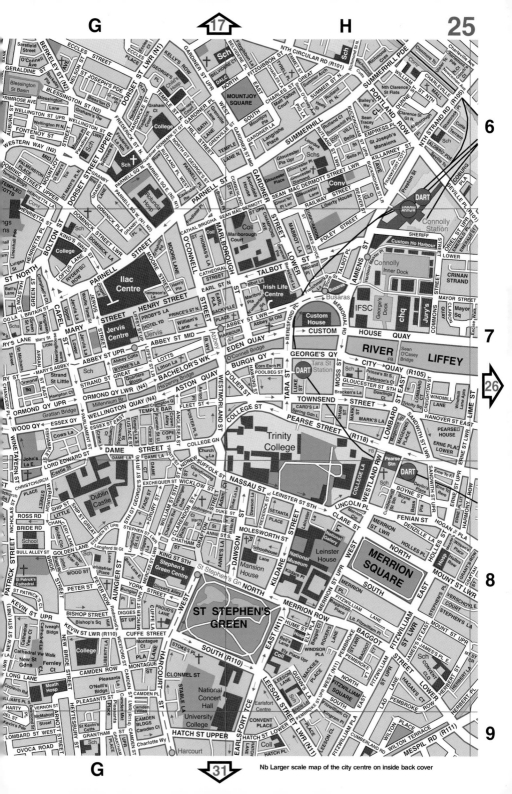

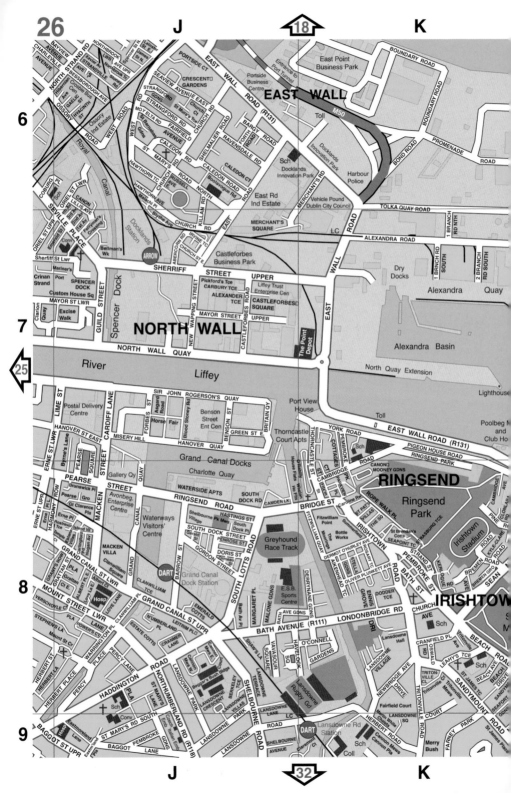

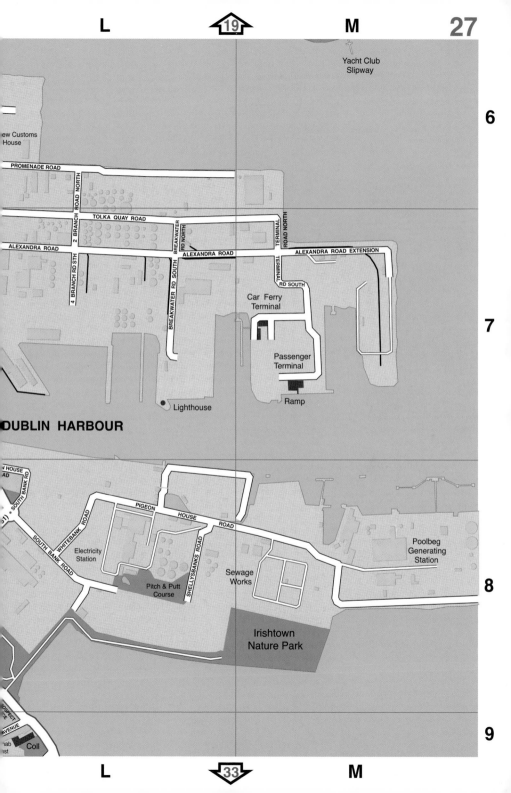

6

Yacht Club
Slipway

ew Customs
House

PROMENADE ROAD

2 BRANCH ROAD NORTH

TOLKA QUAY ROAD

ALEXANDRA ROAD

4 BRANCH RD STH

BREAKWATER RD NORTH

BREAKWATER RD SOUTH

ALEXANDRA ROAD

TERMINAL ROAD NORTH

ALEXANDRA ROAD EXTENSION

TERMINAL RD SOUTH

Car Ferry
Terminal

7

Passenger
Terminal

Lighthouse

Ramp

DUBLIN HARBOUR

N HOUSE
AD

SOUTH BANK RD

PIGEON   HOUSE   ROAD

WHITEBANK ROAD

SOUTH BANK ROAD

SHELLYSBANKS ROAD

Electricity
Station

Pitch & Putt
Course

Sewage
Works

Poolbeg
Generating
Station

8

Irishtown
Nature Park

ADOSPECT

AVENUE
st

hab   Coll

9

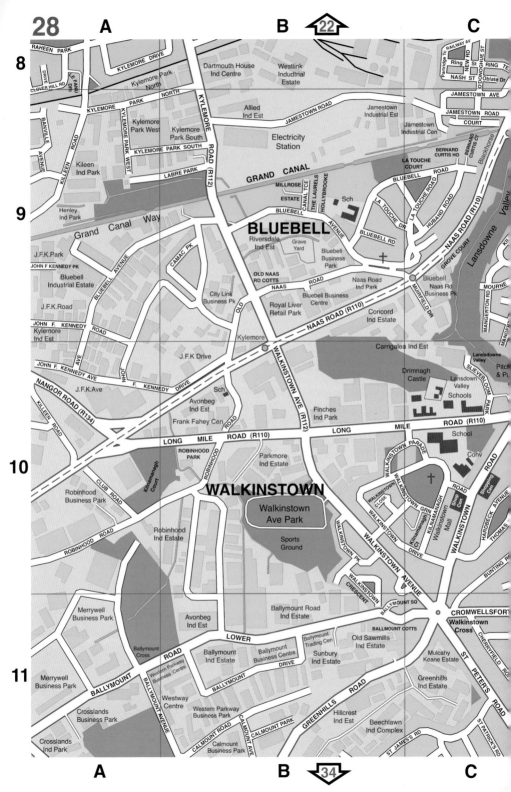

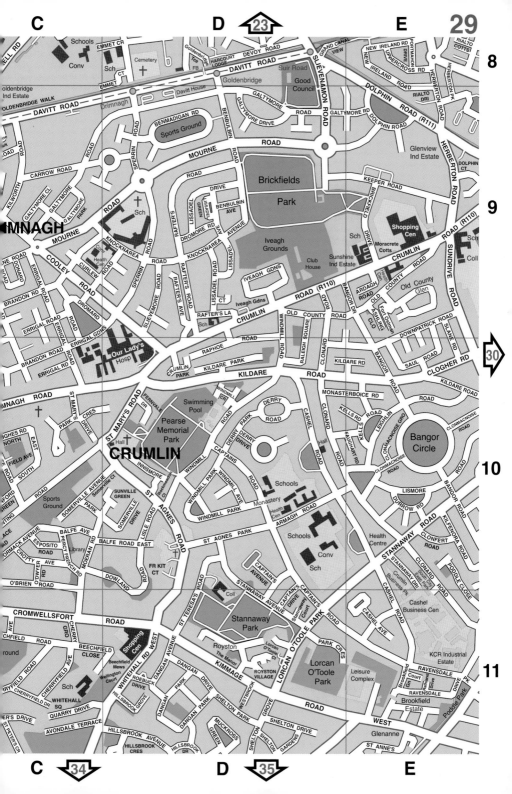

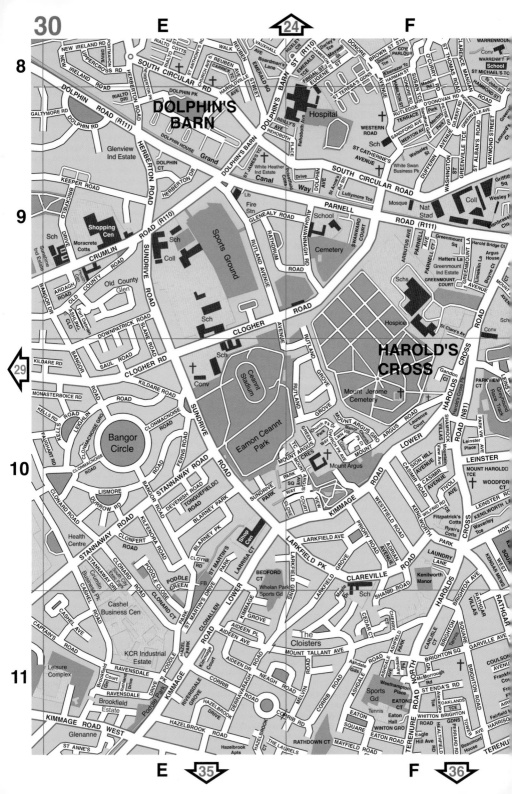

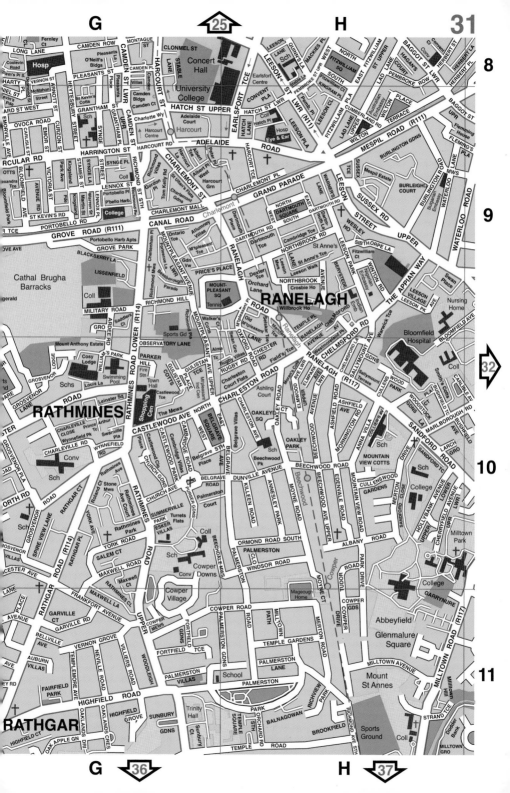

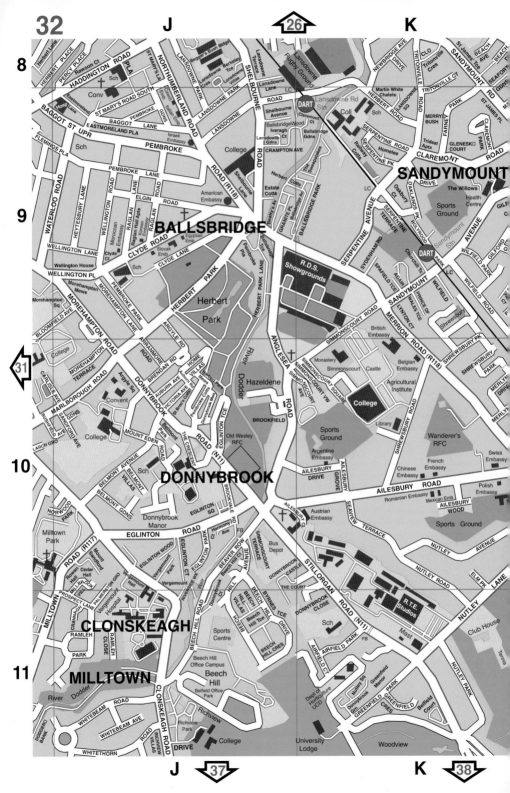

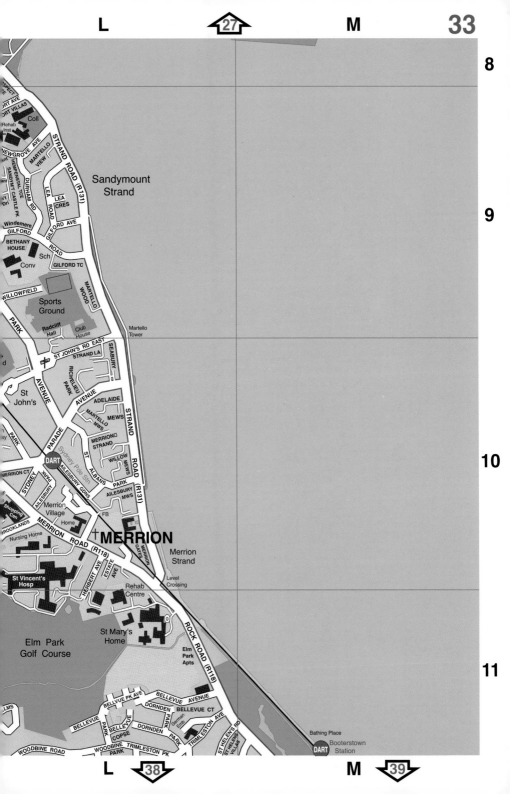

8

9

10

11

RT AVE

ORT VILLAS

Rehab
Inst

Coll

NEWGROVE

MARTELLO AVE

DURHAM RD

STRAND AVE

STRAND ROAD (R131)

VIEW

LEA

LEA
CRES

GILFORD AVE

GILFORD AVE

Sandymount
Strand

Windemere

GILFORD

BETHANY
HOUSE

ROAD

Sch

Conv

GILFORD TC

WILLOWFIELD

MARTELLO
WOOD

PARK

Sports
Ground

Radcliff
Hall

Club
House

Martello
Tower

St JOHN'S RD EAST

STRAND LA

SEABURY

RICHELIEU
PARK

AVENUE

ADELAIDE

St
John's

AVENUE

MARTELLO
MWS

MEWS

STRAND

MERRION
STRAND

WILLOW
MEWS

PARADE

PARK

DART

Sydney Pde Stn

ST ALBANS

AILESBURY GDNS

AILESBURY
MWS

MERRION CT

SYDNEY

PARK

AILESBURY

Merrion
Village

FB

Shopping
Ctr

Home

BROOKLANDS

Nursing Home

MERRION ROAD (R118)

✝ **MERRION**

MERRION
GATES

Merrion
Strand

St Vincent's
Hosp

HERBERT AVE

ESTATE

AVE

Rehab
Centre

Level
Crossing

Elm Park
Golf Course

St Mary's
Home

ROCK ROAD (R118)

Elm
Park
Apts

BELLVUE PK AVE

BELLEVUE   AVENUE

DORNDEN

BELLEVUE CT

LMS

BELLEVUE

PARK

BELLEVUE

COPSE

DORNDEN

PARK

German
Emb

TRIMLESTON AVE

WOODBINE ROAD

WOODBINE
PARK

TRIMLESTON PK

ST HELEN'S RD

Bathing Place

DART Booterstown
Station

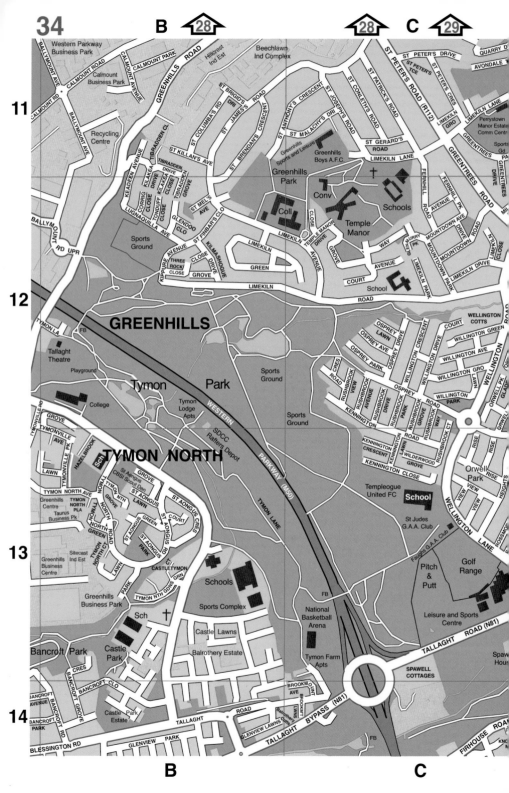

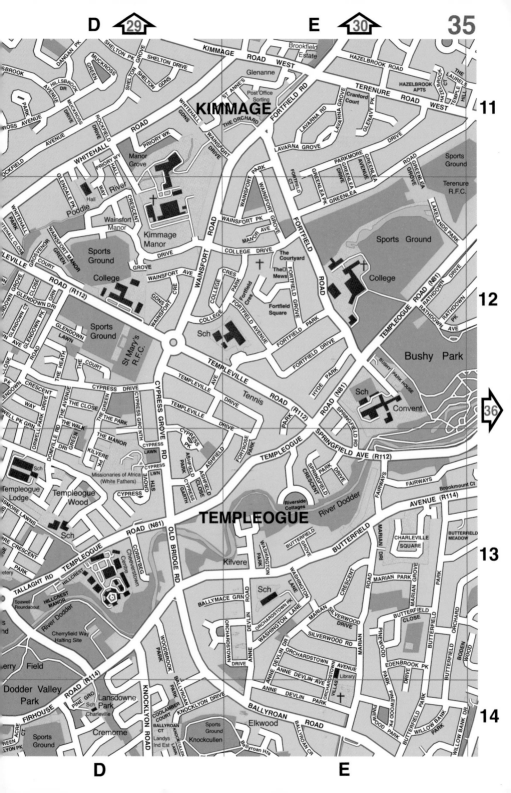

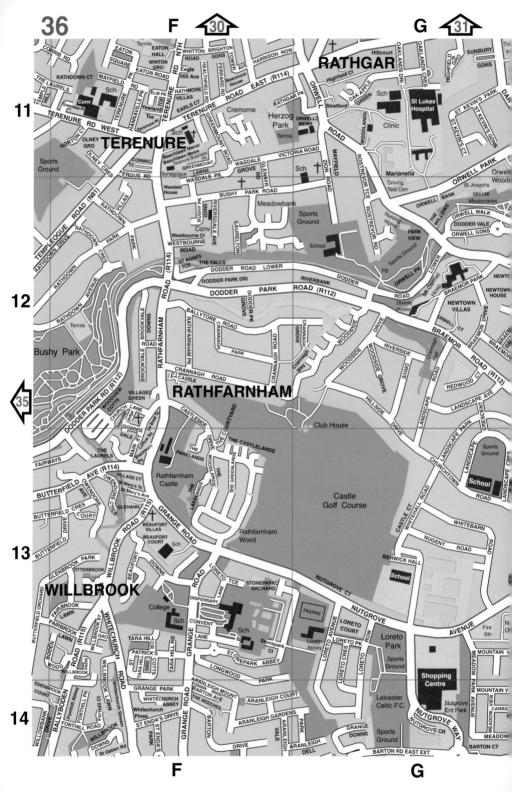

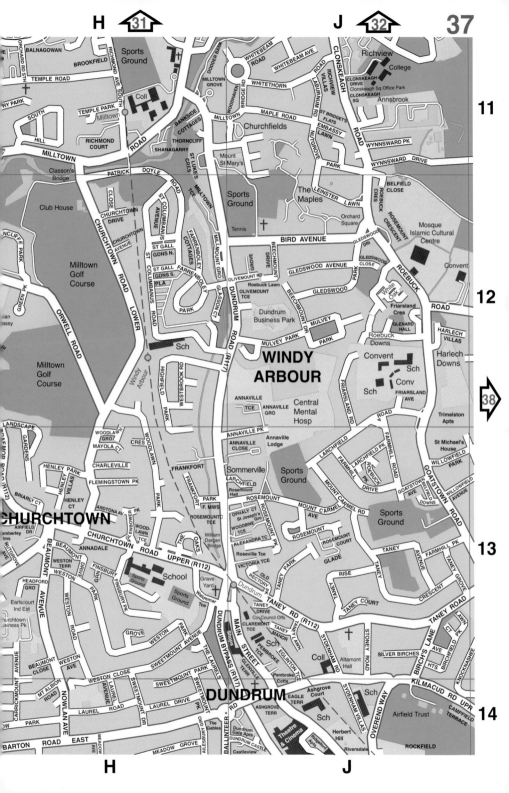

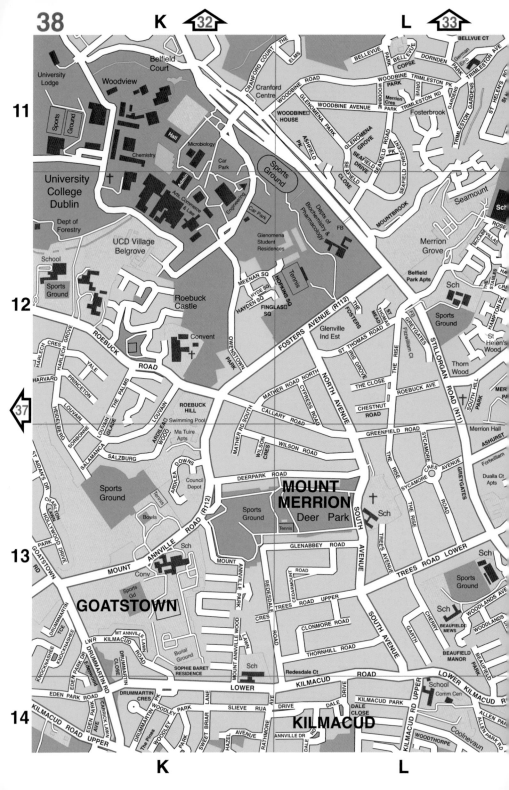

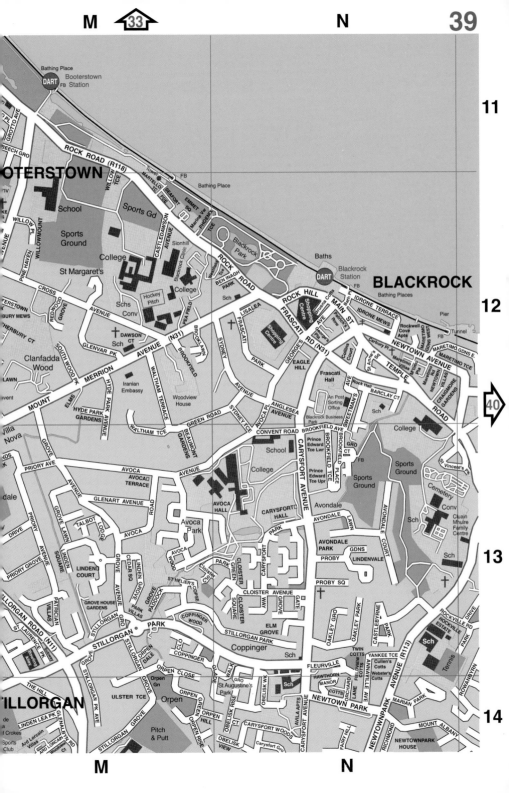

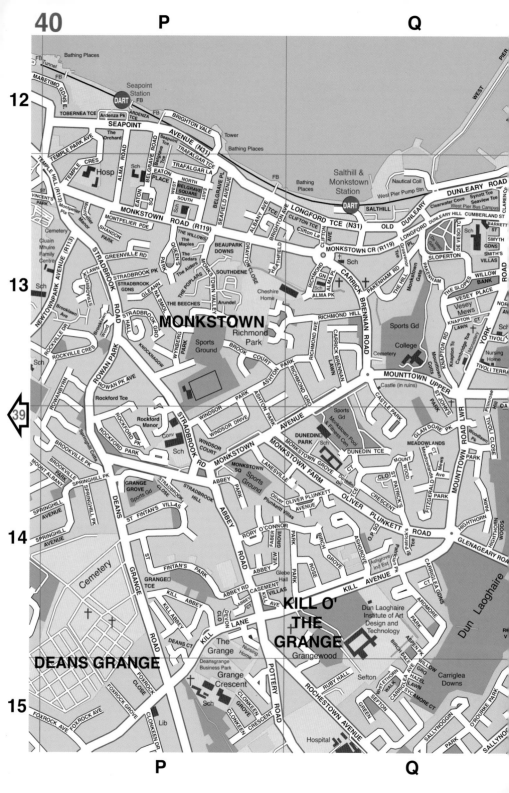

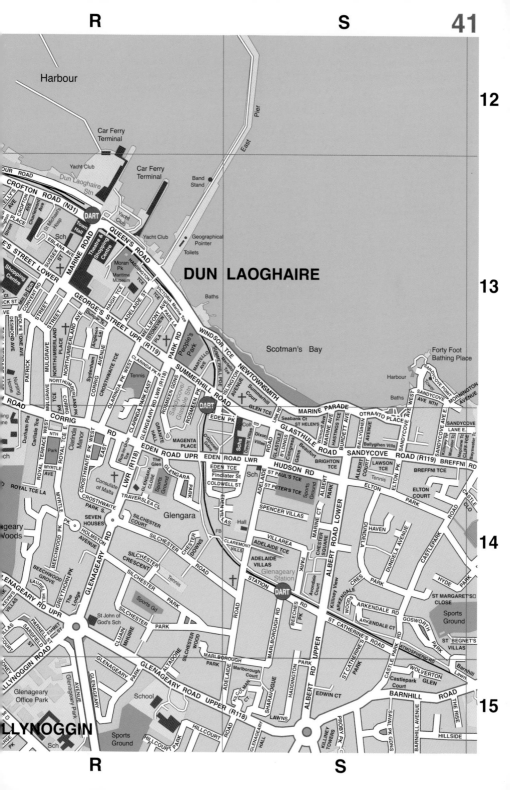

12

13

14

15

Harbour

East Pier

Car Ferry Terminal

Yacht Club

Dun Laoghaire Stn

Car Ferry Terminal

Band Stand

CROFTON ROAD (N31)

DART

Town Hall

Sch

Hosp

St Michaels

Yacht Club

Theatre & Shopping Centre

Queen's Road

MARINE ROAD

Geographical Pointer

Toilets

DUN LAOGHAIRE

Moran Pk

Maritime Museum

Baths

Scotman's Bay

GEORGE'S STREET UPR

GEORGE'S STREET LOWER

Shopping Centre

People's Park

WINDSOR TCE

NEWTOWNSMITH

SUMMERHILL ROAD

Tennis

DART

EDEN PK

MARINE PARADE

Seabank Ct

ST HELEN'S

MARINE AVE

HASTINGS TCE

OTRANTO PLACE

Harbour

Baths

Forty Foot Bathing Place

SANDYCOVE AVE WEST

SANDYCOVE AVE NTH

MORNINGTON AVENUE

SANDYCOVE AVE E.

SANDYCOVE LANE E.

CORRIG RD

MAGENTA PLACE

GLASTHULE ROAD

SANDYCOVE ROAD (R119)

BREFFNI RD

BREFFNI TCE

Dixon Villas

Villas

BRIGHTON TCE

HUDSON RD

SANDYCOVE

LAWSON TCE

ELTON PARK

ELTON COURT

EDEN ROAD UPR

EDEN ROAD LWR

ST PAUL'S TCE

ST PETER'S TCE

Sch

ALBERT COURT

Findlater St

COLDWELL ST

The Glen

Glengara

SPENCER VILLAS

ALBERT ROAD LOWER

DUNDELA AVENUE

HAVEN

CASTLEPARK

HYDE PARK

CROSTHWAITE PK WEST

CROSTHWAITE PARK S.

Glengara

TRAVERSLEA CL

Hall

VILLAREA

ADELAIDE TCE

MARINE CT

CHESTER SQUARE

CRES

PARK

ST MARGARET'S CLOSE

SEVEN HOUSES

SILCHESTER COURT

CHESTER DOWNS

CLAREMONT VILLS

ADELAIDE VILLAS

PARK

Avondale Court

Killiney View

ARKENDALE RD

WOODS

ARKENDALE CT

Sports Ground

GOSWORTH PARK

ST BEGNET'S VILLAS

GLENAGEARY RD UPR

SILCHESTER CRESCENT

SILCHESTER PARK

Tennis

ROAD

Glengeary Station

DART

BEECHES PK

MARLBOROUGH RD

ST CATHERINE'S ROAD

CASTLE PARK

ATMOSPHERIC RD

WOLVERTON GLEN

Barnhill Lawn

The Lodge

St John of God's Sch

SILCHESTER PARK

PARK

SILCHESTER WOOD

ALTADORE

MARLBOROUGH PARK

Marlborough Court

ADELAIDE ROAD

SHARAVOGUE

HADDINGTON PARK

ST CATHERINE'S PARK

ALBERT RD UPPER

EDWIN CT

Castlepark Court

BARNHILL ROAD

THE RISE

GLENAGEARY ROAD UPPER (R118)

School

HILLCOURT ROAD

LAWNS

KILLINEY TOWERS

PROBY PK

NAVAL PK

BARNHILL AVENUE

SAVAL PK GDNS

HILLSIDE

Glenageary Office Park

Sports Ground

HILLCOURT PARK

Sch

LLYNOGGIN

STREET INDEX

Due to insufficient space, some streets and/or their names have been omitted from the street map. Street names below which are prefixed by a * are not represented on the map, but they can be located by referring in the index to the name of the street which follows in brackets.

Page	Grid Ref	Page	Grid Ref	Page	Grid Ref	Page	Grid Ref

25 ABBEY COTTS. G7
9 Abbey Court L4
40 Abbey Court P14
(Monkstown)
15 Abbey Drive D5
11 Abbey Park (Baldoyle) Q2
40 Abbey Park P14
(Kill of the Grange)
9 Abbey Park L4
40 Abbey Road P14
13 Abbey Street (Howth) V2
25 Abbey Street, Lower H7
25 Abbey Street, Middle G7
25 Abbey Street, Old H7
25 Abbey Street, Upper G7
13 *Abbey Tce V2
(off Abbey St)
40 Abbey View P14
9 Abbeyfield L4
31 Abbeyfield H11
5 Abbotstown Avenue C3
5 Abbotstown Drive D3
5 Abbotstown Road D3
26 Abercorn Road J7
23 Abercorn Square C8
23 Abercorn Terrace C8
24 Aberdeen Street E7
17 Achill Road H4
22 Acres Road L4
32 Adair K9
25 *Adair Lane G7
(off Aston Quay)
17 *Adair Terrace G6
(Dorset St. Upper)
25 Adam Court G8
9 Adare Avenue L2
9 Adare Drive L2
9 Adare Green L2
9 Adare Park L2
9 Adare Road L2
6 *Addison Avenue F4
(Addison Lane)
6 Addison Drive F4
6 *Addison Hall F4
(Addison Lane)
6 Addison Lane F4
17 Addison Place G4
18 Addison Road J5
31 Adelaide Court G9
33 Adelaide Mews L10
41 Adelaide Road S14
(Dun Laoghaire)
31 Adelaide Road G9
(Leeson Street)
41 Adelaide Street R13
41 Adelaide Terrace S14
(Dun Laoghaire)
23 Adelaide Terrace E8
41 Adelaide Villas S14
11 Admiral Park R1
11 Admiral Ct R1
30 Adrian Avenue F10
30 Aideen Avenue E11
30 Aideen Place E11
26 Aikenhead Terrace K8
7 Ailesbury H2
32 Ailesbury Close J10
32 Ailesbury Drive K10
33 Ailesbury Gardens L10
32 Ailesbury Grove K10
(Donnybrook)
32 *Ailesbury Lane K10
(off Ailesbury Road)
33 Ailesbury Mews L10
33 Ailesbury Park L10
32 Ailesbury Road K10
32 Ailesbury Wood K10
32 Airfield Court K11
37 Airfield Drive H13
32 Airfield Park K11
30 Airfield Road F11
30 Aisling Close E9
40 Albany Avenue P13
31 Albany Road H10
7 Albert College Avenue G3
7 Albert College Court. G3
7 Albert College Cres. G3

7 Albert College Drive G3
7 Albert College Gro. G3
7 Albert College Lawn G3
7 Albert College Park G3
41 Albert Court S14
26 Albert Court J8
41 Albert Park S14
26 Albert Place East J8
31 Albert Place, West G9
41 Albert Road Lower S14
41 Albert Road Upper S15
31 Albert Terrace G9
41 *Albert Terrace R13
(Crofton Rd, Dun
Laoghaire)
17 Aldborough Pde. H6
17 Aldborough Place H6
17 *Aldborough Square H6
(off Aldborough Place)
11 Alden Drive Q2
11 Alden Park Q2
11 Alden Road Q2
9 Aldrin Walk L2
37 Alesbury Grove H14
26 Alexander Terrace J7
(North Wall)
37 *Alexandra Court J13
(Woodbine Terrace)
26 Alexandra Quay K7
26 *Alexandra Quay K7
(off York Road)
26 Alexandra Road K7
27 Alexandra Road Ext M7
37 Alexandra Terrace J13
(Dundrum)
31 Alexandra Terrace G9
(Portobello)
30 Alexandra Terrace F11
(Terenure)
37 *Alexandra Villas J13
(Alexandra Tce)
18 Alfie Byrne Road J6
17 All Hallows Green H4
17 All Hallows Square H4
10 All Saints Close N4
10 All Saints Drive N4
10 All Saints Park N4
9 All Saints Road M4
38 Allen Park Drive L14
38 Allen Park Road L14
24 Allingham Street F8
40 Alma Park Q13
40 Alma Place Q13
40 Alma Road P13
31 Alma Terrace G10
24 Almeida Avenue E8
24 Almeida Terrace E8
9 Alone Walk L3
19 Alverno L6(1)
25 Amiens Street H7
39 Anglesea Avenue N12
41 Anglesea Lane R13
32 Anglesea Road J10
25 Anglesea Row G7
25 Anglesea Street G7
35 Ann Devlin Avenue E13
35 Ann Devlin Drive E13
35 Ann Devlin Park E14
35 Ann Devlin Road E13
31 Anna Villa H10
37 Annadale H13
18 Annadale Avenue J5
18 Annadale Crescent J4
18 Annadale Drive J4
16 Annaly Road F5
16 Annamoe Drive F6
16 Annamoe Parade F6
16 Annamoe Park F6
16 Annamoe Road E6
16 Annamoe Terrace F6
39 Annaville Avenue N13
37 Annaville Close J12
37 Annaville Grove J12
37 Annaville Lodge J12
37 Annaville Park J12
37 Annaville Terrace J12
25 Anne Street, North G7
25 Anne Street, South G8

25 Anne's Lane G8
23 Anner Road D8
18 Annesley Avenue J6
18 Annesley Bridge Road J5
31 Annesley Park H10
18 Annesley Place J6
37 Annsbrook J11
38 Annville Drive L14
8 Apollo Way K2
31 *Appian Close H9
(on Leeson Park)
36 Aranleigh Court F14
36 Aranleigh Dell G14
36 Aranleigh Gardens F14
36 Aranleigh Mount F14
36 Aranleigh Park F14
36 Aranleigh Vale F14
24 Arbour Hill F7
24 Arbour Place F7
24 Arbour Terrace E7
30 Arbutus Avenue F9
31 Arbutus Place G9
39 Ard Lorcain M14
39 Ard Lorcain Villas M14
7 Ard na Meala G1
24 Ard-Righ Place F7
24 Ard-Ri Road F7
30 Ardagh Road E9
9 Ardara Avenue N1
9 Ardbeg Crescent L3
9 Ardbeg Drive L3
9 Ardbeg Park L3
9 Ardbeg Road L3
9 Ardcollum Avenue L3
31 Ardee Grove G9
31 Ardee Road G9
24 Ardee Row F8
24 Ardee Street F8
40 Ardenza Park P12
40 Ardenza Terrace P12
17 Ardilaun Road H6
17 *Ardilaun Square H6
(off Sackville Avenue)
38 Ardilea Downs K13
38 Ardilea Wood K13
9 Ardlea Road L3
16 Ardmore Avenue E6
8 Ardmore Close K3
8 Ardmore Crescent K3
8 Ardmore Drive K2
8 Ardmore Grove K2
8 Ardmore Park K3
8 *Ardmore Park K3
(Artane)
40 Ardmore Park Q14
(Kill of the Grange)
15 Ardpatrick Road D5
37 Ardtona Avenue H13
30 Argus House F9
32 Argyle Road J9
32 Argyle Square J10
41 Arkendale Court S14
41 Arkendale Road S14
41 Arkendale Woods S14
16 Arklow Street E6
29 Armagh Road D10
30 *Armstrong Street F10
(off Harold's Cross Road)
9 Armstrong Walk L2
23 Army Road D7
25 Arnott Street G8
24 Arran Quay F7
24 Arran Quay Terr. F7
25 Arran Street, East G7
7 Arran Street West F7
17 Arranmore Avenue G6
32 Arranmore Road J10
9 Artane L3
9 Artane Cotts. Lower L3
9 Artane Cotts. Upper L3
40 Arundel P13
25 *Asdill's Row G7
(off Temple Bar)
13 Asgard Apartments V2
24 Asgard Park V3
13 Asgard Road V3
24 Asgard Road J7
24 *Ash Grove F8

(Meath Street)
24 Ash Street F8
19 Ashbrook L5
14 Ashbrook C4
31 *Ashbrook Terrace H10
(Ranelagh)
31 *Ashbrook Villas H10
(Ranelagh)
10 Ashcroft N3
30 Ashdale Avenue F11
30 Ashdale Gardens F11
30 Ashdale Park F11
30 Ashdale Road F11
(Terenure)
35 Ashfeld D13
31 Ashfield Avenue H10
(Ranelagh)
35 Ashfield Close D13
(Templeogue)
38 Ashfield Park L11
(Booterstown)
35 Ashfield Park D13
(Templeogue)
30 Ashfield Park F11
(Terenure)
31 Ashfield Road H10
(Ranelagh)
16 *Ashford Cottages E6
(off Ashford Street)
16 *Ashford Place E6
(off Ashford Street)
16 Ashford Street E6
40 Ashgrove Q14
(Kill of the Grange)
37 Ashgrove Court J14
37 Ashgrove Terrace J14
15 Ashington Avenue D4
15 Ashington Close D4
15 Ashington Court D4
15 Ashington Crescent C4
15 Ashington Dale D4
15 Ashington Gardens D4
15 Ashington Green D4
15 Ashington Grove D4
15 Ashington Heath D4
15 Ashington Mews D4
15 Ashington Park D4
15 Ashington Rise C4
30 Ashling Close E9
31 Ashling Court H10
23 Ashmount Court D8
40 Ashton Park P3
14 Ashtown C4
14 Ashtown Gate Road B5
15 Ashtown Grove C5
15 Ashtown Lodge C5
14 Ashtown Road B4
14 Ashtowngate B4
38 Ashurst L13
30 *Ashworth Place F9
(off Mount Drumond Ave.)
24 Aspen Park Q14
25 Aston Place G7
25 Aston Quay G7
31 Atlumney Villas G9
41 Atmospheric Road S14
18 Auburn K5
32 Auburn Avenue J10
(Donnybrook)
32 Auburn Road J10
(Donnybrook)
17 Auburn Street G6
31 Auburn Villas G11
16 Auburn Walk E6
30 Aughavannagh Road F9
16 Aughrim Court F6
16 Aughrim Lane F6
16 Aughrim Place E6
16 Aughrim Street E6
16 Aughrim Villas E6
8 Aulden Grange J1
25 Aungier Lane G8
25 Aungier Place G8
25 Aungier Street G8
18 Austin's Cottages J6
12 Avalon Apts T2
24 Ave Maria Road E8
31 Avenue Road G9

STREET INDEX

STREET INDEX

46

STREET INDEX

STREET INDEX

STREET INDEX

STREET INDEX

STREET INDEX

STREET INDEX

STREET INDEX

STREET INDEX

Dublin gets its name from the Gaelic, *dubh linn*, which means dark pool, a reference to the spot where the River Liffey meets the River Poddle. The first settlement near to this spot dates back more than 5,000 years.

Christianity arrived with Saint Patrick in 432 AD, and a golden age of Gaelic Christianity followed which produced magnificent works of religious art such as the Book of Kells which can still be seen today at Trinity College.

The native population remained largely undisturbed by further foreign visitors until the Vikings arrived early in the 9th century. Despite fierce resistance from the native Irish, the Norsemen consolidated their presence with victory in the Battle of Dublin in 919 and the town subsequently became an important trading post in the Viking empire.

The Vikings were finally overcome by the Gaelic clans at the Battle of Clontarf in 1014 but their influence is still marked today by place names such as Howth, from the Norse word *hovud* meaning headland, and Leixlip, from the Norse word *laxlep* meaning salmon leap.

The next invaders were Anglo Normans sent by King Henry II. Led by the Earl of Pembroke, who was better known as Strongbow, they landed in Wexford in 1169. Dublin was soon overwhelmed by the strength of their forces and the Normans quickly set about changing the urban landscape. Henry granted the town a charter in 1171 and established court there. The oldest surviving buildings in the city date from this period, including Christ Church and Saint Patrick's cathedrals, and parts of Dublin Castle. Due to the fact that wood was the main component of their con-

struction, however, very little of the original buildings remain for us to see today.

English customs and the English language prevailed in and around the city, within an area which became known as the Pale, but Irish chieftains held sway elsewhere, giving rise to the phrase 'beyond the Pale'. By 1542, Henry VIII had proclaimed himself King of Ireland as well as England, and the Reformation came to Ireland. Dublin became Protestant, and grew in importance as royal authority spread to other parts of Ireland. By 1592 the College of the Holy and Undivided Trinity of Queen Elizabeth was founded on land confiscated from the Priory of All Hallows. Commonly known as Trinity College, this Protestant seat of learning has played an illustrious role in Dublin's history over the past 400 years.

With Charles I beheaded and the English monarchy abolished, Oliver Cromwell landed in Dublin with a large army in 1649, ushering in a particularly bloody and savage era in Irish history. After the restoration of the monarchy in 1660, Dublin began to take on much of the shape which we recognise today. St Stephen's Green and the Phoenix Park were laid out and many significant public buildings were erected including the Royal Hospital in Kilmainham, now the Museum of Modern Art.

By 1688, Catholic King James II had been deposed in favour of his daughter, Mary, who ruled jointly with her Protestant husband, William of Orange. Ireland was set to become a battlefield for a religious war involving most of Europe's major powers. In 1690 James lost the Battle of the Boyne to King William, and Catholics subsequently suffered under the Penal Laws. Gaelic cul-

ture was driven underground and the seeds were sewn for the struggle for Irish autonomy from England.

The 18th century ushered in a golden age for Dublin, and the city flourished both physically and culturally. Parliament House (now the Bank of Ireland), Custom House, the Mansion House, the Four Courts and Marsh's Library were all built during this period. Jonathan Swift, the author of *Gulliver's Travels*, returned to the city in 1713 to become Dean of St Patrick's Cathedral, and Handel came to Dublin to give the first performance of his *Messiah* in 1742.

This golden age was short lived, however. The Act of Union of 1800 brought Ireland into a United Kingdom with Britain, and the seat of political power moved from Dublin to Westminster. The city's aristocracy followed and Dublin lost much of its social and cultural sparkle.

A century of political turmoil followed. Daniel O'Connell helped to achieve Catholic emancipation in 1829 and, as a Catholic middle class developed, Dublin started to become a distinctly Irish city. The city managed to escape the worst effects of the potato famine which decimated much of Ireland in the late 1840's, and it expanded rapidly as migrants flooded in from the surrounding countryside. But the effect of the famine on the country as a whole was devastating. Out of a population of 8.5 million, approximately one million starved to death and a further 1.5 million emigrated, mainly to Britain and North America. The famine years served to heighten anti-British sentiment, and an abortive rebellion by the Irish Republican Brotherhood in 1868 led to calls for Irish Home Rule.

The case for Irish autonomy was taken up in the English parliament at Westminster by the Protestant leader, Charles Stewart Parnell. When Parnell died in 1891, he left a political vacuum which was eventually filled by two cultural movements, the Gaelic League which was set up to revive the Irish Language, and the Irish Literary Renaissance. William Butler Yeats played a pivotal role in restoring national pride with the foundation of the Abbey Theatre in 1904, giving prominence to playwrights such as Sean O'Casey and J. M. Synge. This cultural nationalism developed into political nationalism with the establishment of Sinn Féin (Ourselves Alone), a political movement which advocated a boycott of the English parliament. With Britain engaged in the First World War, Sinn Féin organised the occupation of several strategic buildings around Dublin, and declared an Irish republic from its headquarters in the General Post Office on Easter Monday 1916.

Dublin's financial district has changed the face of the River Liffey

The Easter Rising was quashed after six days of fighting that involved 20,000 British troops, and 15 of the rebel leaders were later executed. A wave of public sympathy resulted, and Sinn Féin secured an overwhelming victory in the 1918 elections. A War of Independence between British and Irish republican armies soon followed and, after two years of fighting, General Michael Collins signed a treaty in 1921 which resulted in the creation of the Irish Free State, comprising 26 of Ireland's 32 counties. The other six counties became known as Northern Ireland and remained within the United Kingdom. Collins said at the time that he was signing his own death warrant, and he was proved right a year later when he was assassinated.

The treaty caused division between different factions within Sinn Féin and a bitter Civil War broke out which lasted for a year and saw the destruction of much of the city. Eamon de Valera won the battle for political control of the new state, and a period of political and cultural conservatism ensued which lasted until the late 1950's.

Ireland was declared a republic in 1949, but it was not until the 1960's that Dublin started to look outward. De Valera stepped down in 1959 to assume the figurehead role of Irish President, and a new *Taoiseach* (Prime Minister), Sean Lemass, assumed power and began the process of modernisation and industrialisation. Perhaps the most defining moment in Dublin's recent history, however, was Ireland's admission to the European Economic Community in 1973.

Over the past thirty years, Ireland has been transformed from a predominantly agricultural country into a vibrant industrial economy. Dublin today is a modern European capital which boasts a young and well educated population which has proved attractive to many foreign investors. Church and Government are becoming increasingly disentangled as evidenced by the 1995 referendum result in favour of divorce, and liberalisation of laws in relation to homosexuality and abortion.

The Government's initiative in setting up the International Financial Services Centre in the heart of the city has succeeded in attracting many of the world's leading investment banks, making Dublin an important offshore financial centre. Ireland is also at the cutting edge in electronics and information technology, ranking second only to the USA as an exporter of computer software, supplying around 40% of the European market. Economic progress during the 1990's was startling, and by the turn of the millennium the Celtic Tiger was enjoying an income per head which exceeded that of the UK for the first time

Irish Famine memorial on Custom House Quay

in Irish history.

This process of modernisation has brought problems as well as benefits, though. Drug culture and organised crime have prospered alongside the rest of the economy, despite the war waged against them by the police. Corruption in business and government has become a long running soap opera in the shape of the public tribunals set up to investigate some very shady dealings.

After centuries of dispersing its citizens around the world, Ireland has become a magnet for economic migrants, resulting in a new air of multi-culturalism. More than ten per cent of the current population was born overseas, a fact that is not universally welcomed.

Health and education services are being stretched very thinly. Congestion has reached the point where driving through Dublin takes place at a pace somewhere between slow and stop. The Luas tram system, the Dublin Port Tunnel, and the completion of the M50 motorway have provided some relief but, just as things looked like they were starting to move, the Celtic Tiger has suddenly lost its roar.

After 25 years of economic growth, Ireland is experiencing recession. In their rejection of the Lisbon Treaty which advocated further political integration, Irish voters bit the European hand which helped to fatten them. The Government has had to step in to save the Irish banking system from financial meltdown in the face of a global credit crunch, and the country's overvalued property market is facing a grim reality check. After one heck of a party, uncertainty reigns although a painful hangover looks inevitable.

Thankfully, though, Dublin retains much of its Georgian charm and grandeur. For a city with a population of around one million people, it is compact and intimate, with many of its attractions within walking distance of one another. This factor, together with its rich literary tradition and reputation for youthful exuberance and a friendly welcome, means that it remains one of the world's favourite tourist destinations.

Whether you are living here or merely passing through, the sections which follow will try to help you make the best of all that Dublin has to offer.

AIR TRAVEL

Dublin Airport, which lies about 7 miles north of the city centre, is Ireland's main international gateway with nearly 100 airlines serving around 200 routes. Aer Lingus is Ireland's national carrier, operating several domestic services out of Dublin in addition to its international routes. **Dublin Airport Authority**, the airport managers, provide a comprehensive flight information service. Telephone 814 1111 or visit their web site at www.dublinairport.com.

International and domestic arrivals and departures share the same terminal building - arrivals are upstairs and departures are downstairs. The airport handles 24 million passengers annually and can feel rather chaotic at times, partly due to an ongoing €2bn investment program. A second terminal is due to open in 2010 which should relieve the strain. Facilities include bureaux de change, a bank, post office, national bus and rail information desk (CIE), and a very good tourist information office downstairs, as well as a much improved array of bars, restaurants, cafés and shops. The tourist information office is a good first stop to find your bearings, and make reservations if you have not already booked accommodation.

Dublin Bus operates an express bus service called **Airlink** which departs from outside the arrivals hall. Service number 747 stops in the city centre on O'Connell Street before going on to Busáras, the central bus station, which is only a couple of minutes walk from Connolly railway station. Service 748 stops at Busáras, before continuing on to Heuston railway station. Frequency of departures varies from ten to twenty minutes depending on the time of day. The first service is at 5.45am, and the last at 11.30pm; the single fare is €6. Tickets can be bought from the CIE Information Desk in the arrivals hall, or on board the bus, and the journey into town normally takes around half an hour, depending on traffic (allow an extra 15 minutes to Heuston Station).

Aircoach offers an alternative service which takes in the city centre, Ballsbridge and Donnybrook, stopping at many of Dublin's major hotels. Coaches leave every 10 or 20 minutes from 4.30am until 12.30am, and hourly from 12.30am to 4.30am. Tickets, which cost €7 single and €12 return, can be bought at the bus stop outside the terminal building. Up to two children under 5 can travel free if accompanied by a fare paying adult. Kids between the ages of 5 and 12 travel for a flat fee of €1. Other destinations served by Aircoach include Leopardstown, Greystones, Belfast and Cork.

Dublin Bus numbers 41 and 16A offer cheaper travel into the city centre but journey times are longer as these are normal suburban services. Similarly, Dublin Bus number 746 offers a cheap means of reaching areas south of the city, such as Donnybrook, Stillorgan and Dun Laoghaire, without having to change buses in the centre of town. Services depart from in front of the arrivals hall.

If you are trying to get farther afield, **Bus Éireann** operates services from the airport to Belfast, Derry and Letterkenny; **J J Kavanagh** provide services to Limerick and Waterford; **Ardcavan** provides a service to Wexford; and **GoBus** and **Citylink** provide services to Galway.

A cab from the taxi rank in front of the terminal building will take you into the city centre for around €25 (no extra charge for the wise-cracking which tends to be the hallmark of Dublin cabbies).

Avis, Budget, Hertz Europcar and **National** all have car hire desks in the arrivals concourse, and a number of other operators, including **Argus, Atlas, Dan Dooley,** and **Thrifty,** provide cars which must be booked before your arrival. Given that life behind the steering wheel in Dublin is often a frustrating one, and that the city centre is a very walkable one, you might well wonder why you bothered to hire a car in the first place!

FERRY SERVICES

There are two ferry ports in Dublin. **Dublin Port** is situated just a couple of miles from the city centre on Alexandra Road in an area known as the North Wall. **Irish Ferries** operate a ferry crossing to Holyhead in North Wales which takes just over three hours, or a fast ferry service which completes the same journey in one hour forty five minutes (www.irishferries.com). **Stena Line** also offer a ferry service to Holyhead which takes around three hours (www.stenaline.co.uk). **Norfolkline** operate daily day and night crossings between Dublin Port and Liverpool with a crossing time of approximately 7 hours (norfolkline.com). **P & O Irish Sea** also cross day and night to Liverpool with a journey time of around 8 hours (poirishsea.com). Dublin Bus number 53 will take you the short distance from Dublin Port to town.

Dún Laoghaire Port is 7 miles south of the city centre. Stena Line's HSS service will get you to Holyhead in 99 minutes. The port is easily reached by DART train service or Dublin Bus numbers 7,46A and 746. A DART station is adjacent to the ferry terminal and the trains are fast and frequent. The terminal building has its own tourist information office which offers a useful reservation service if you are in search of accommodation.

TRAINS

Irish rail services, including the **DART,** are operated by **Iarnród Éireann (Irish Rail)**, and their Rail Travel Centre at 35 Lower Abbey Street is a good place to gather information and make bookings. Phone 836 6222 for information on all services or visit their web site at www.irishrail.ie

Inter City Trains

Rail journeys to Belfast, Sligo, Rosslare Europort and Wexford start from **Connolly Station** (see page 25, grid reference H7) which is about ten minutes walk from O'Connell Bridge. Services to Westport, Galway, Limerick, Killarney, Tralee, Cork and Waterford leave from **Heuston Station** (see page 24, grid reference E7) which is a short bus or Luas ride to the west of the city centre. Bus service number 90 runs every ten minutes between Connolly and Heuston Station, stopping at Busáras, the central bus station, along the way.

The rail network is adequate, covering most major towns and cities, but you will probably have to rely on bus services if you want to reach smaller towns. If you are expecting bullet trains, forget it. Services have been upgraded in recent years, most notably the Dublin to Belfast line, but even inter city trains take about two hours to cover a distance of 100 miles.

Travelling by train tends to cost more than going by bus but there are discounts available for students with a **Student Travelcard** (application forms available from Dublin Bus on O'Connell Street, Irish Rail Travel Centre on Lower Abbey Street, any rail station or students union). The card entitles you to discount travel on rail, bus and Luas services.

A selection of rail and/or bus passes is available to anybody wanting to explore the country as a whole. For example, €138 will buy you an Irish Explorer rail pass which allows 5 days of travel within any 15 day period on all trains within the Republic of Ireland. Phone 836 6222 for further information.

Suburban Trains

Suburban services offer some cheap travel. Trains leaving from Connolly Station head north as far as Dundalk, south as far as Arklow, and northwest as far as Mullingar. Services leaving from Heuston Station head west as far as Kildare (see route map opposite). Some suburban trains use the same track as the DART but they make far fewer stops and therefore offer a good way of making day trips to places such as Malahide, Castletown House in the village of Celbridge, or Newgrange which is near Drogheda.

DART

The DART, or Dublin Area Rapid Transit, is a cheap but excellent electric rail service linking the city centre to various points along the coast of Dublin Bay, as far as Howth and Malahide to the north, and Greystones to the south (see the route map below).

The main city centre stations are Pearse and Tara Street which lie just south of the River Liffey, and Connolly which is just north of the river (see page 25, grid H7). Services operate every 15 minutes (every 5 minutes during the rush hour) from around 6.30am to 11.30pm Monday-Saturday, and less frequently from 9.30am to 11pm on Sunday.

Single fares start at €1.25 but a range of travel passes offer useful savings for frequent users. For instance, a one day travel ticket which is valid for unlimited travel on the DART costs €7.60. A range of combined bus and rail tickets can also be purchased at very little additional cost (see page 64).

Luas

After a long wait, the first phase of Dublin's new Luas tram system is up and running, with the Green Line running south from St Stephen's Green to Sandyford, and the Red Line running southwest from Connolly Station to Tallaght (see route map below). The two lines do not connect, but a ticket bought on one line for a destination on the other is valid. It takes approximately 15 minutes to walk from Abbey Street on the Red Line to St Stephen's Green on the Green line. Single adult fares range from €1.50 to €2.30.

All stops have ticket machines that accept coins, notes and credit cards. Tickets, including weekly and monthly tickets, can also be bought from a network of Luas ticket agents around the city. Dublin Bus ticket agents sell combined bus and Luas tickets that are valid on both networks.

The Luas network will eventually be extended to Lucan, the Point Depot, and to the north of the city. Plans include underground Metro lines which will become part of an integrated urban transport system.

BUS SERVICES

Dublin Buses

Until the future becomes reality, Dubliners will continue to rely primarily on *Bus Átha Cliath* (Dublin Bus) to get them from A to B using a comprehensive bus network which connects the city centre to all of the main suburbs of greater Dublin (see route maps on pages 64 & 65). Destinations and the service number are posted above the driver's window, with buses heading for the city centre displaying the Gaelic words, *An Lár*. Bus stops display the route numbers at the top and also provide additional route information on a revolving carrousel. Travelling by bus is an inexact science, however, and timetables are therefore limited to the departure times from the terminus. Stops that display a "Set Down" sign are for buses which only let passengers off there, so don't wait around in the hope of getting on. The length of the queue at your stop is the best guide as to when the next bus is likely to arrive. Timetables can be obtained from Dublin Bus Head Office at

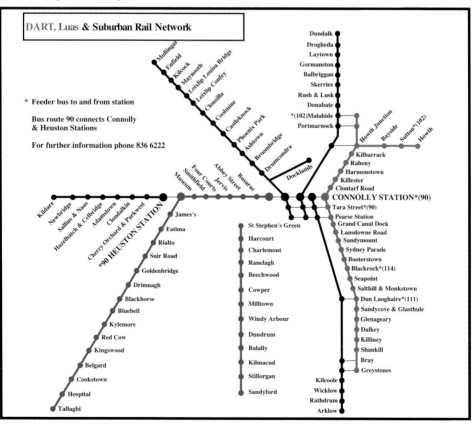

DART, Luas & Suburban Rail Network

* Feeder bus to and from station

Bus route 90 connects Connolly & Heuston Stations

For further information phone 836 6222

Dundalk
Drogheda
Laytown
Gormanston
Balbriggan
Skerries
Rush & Lusk
Donabate
*(102)Malahide
Portmarnock
Howth Junction
Bayside
Sutton*(102)
Howth
Kilbarrack
Raheny
Harmonstown
Killester
Clontarf Road
CONNOLLY STATION*(90)
Tara Street*(90)
Pearse Station
Grand Canal Dock
Lansdowne Road
Sandymount
Sydney Parade
Booterstown
Blackrock*(114)
Seapoint
Salthill & Monkstown
Dun Laoghaire*(111)
Sandycove & Glasthule
Glenageary
Dalkey
Killiney
Shankill
Bray
Greystones
Kilcoole
Wicklow
Rathdrum
Arklow

Mullingar
Enfield
Kilcock
Maynooth
Leixlip Louisa Bridge
Leixlip Confey
Clonsilla
Coolmine
Castleknock
Phoenix Park
Ashtown
Broombridge
Drumcondra
Docklands

Kildare
Newbridge
Sallins & Naas
Hazelhatch & Celbridge
Adamstown
Clondalkin
Cherry Orchard & Parkwest
HEUSTON STATION
*90
James's
Fatima
Rialto
Suir Road
Goldenbridge
Drimnagh
Blackhorse
Bluebell
Kylemore
Red Cow
Kingswood
Belgard
Cookstown
Hospital
Tallaght

Four Courts
Smithfield
Museum
Abbey Street
Jervis
Busaras

St Stephen's Green
Harcourt
Charlemont
Ranelagh
Beechwood
Cowper
Milltown
Windy Arbour
Dundrum
Balally
Kilmacud
Stillorgan
Sandyford

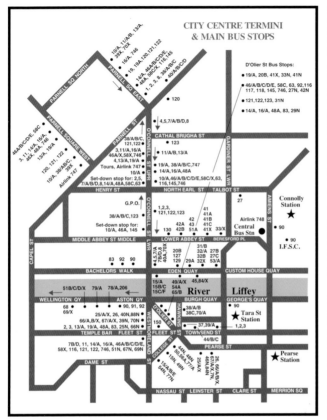

CITY CENTRE TERMINI
& MAIN BUS STOPS

D'Olier St Bus Stops:

● 19/A, 20B, 41X, 33N, 41N

● 46/A/B/C/D/E, 58C, 63, 92,116
117, 118, 145, 746, 27N, 42N

● 121,122,123, 31N

● 14/A, 16/A, 48A, 83, 29N

Seven Day Bus/Rail Ticket

Unlimited travel for one person by Dublin Bus costs €23; by bus and Luas costs €26; by bus, DART and suburban rail costs €31.50

Late Night Buses

Dublin Bus operates a late-night express bus service called **Nitelink** which will get you from the city centre to a wide range of suburban destinations, with up to three pick-up points along the way. Nitelink buses display an 'N' after the route number and services operate every night of the week except for Sundays. Departure points westbound are from Westmoreland Street, northbound from D'Olier St and southbound from College St. Most services depart at 12.30am and 2am Monday to Thursday, and every 30 minutes from 12.30am to 4.30am Friday and Saturday. The fare is €5. You can pay by cash, in coins only, on the bus, or purchase a pre-paid ticket from one of the yellow ticket buses located on the streets from where the services depart. Travel passes are not valid on Nitelink buses. For further information contact 873 4222.

National Bus Service

Bus Eireann (Irish Bus) is the national bus company, operating routes which cover the whole of Ireland. Fares, as a rule, are cheaper than going by train. All buses depart from Busáras, the central bus station, which is situated behind Custom House on Store Street (see page 25, grid H7). Tickets and information are available at Busáras or from the Bus Eireann desk in the Dublin Tourism Centre on Suffolk Street. Phone 836 6111 for more information or visit their web site at www.buseireann.ie.

Bus Tours

Dublin Bus operates a range of daily tours all year round, but with increased frequency during the summer months. **The Dublin City Tour** (from an open-topped double decker, weather permitting!) lasts for an hour and fifteen minutes and leaves from outside Dublin Bus HQ on O'Connell Street. Stops include the Dublin Writers Museum, Trinity College, the National Gallery, St Stephen's Green, Dublin Tourism Centre, Dublin Castle, Christ Church Cathedral, St Patrick's Cathedral, Guinness Storehouse, the Museum of Modern Art, Dublin Zoo, the National Museum, and the Old Jameson Distillery. The tour runs at frequent intervals, normally every ten minutes, between 9.30am and 6.30pm. Tickets, which cost €15 per adult and €6 per child under 14, are valid for 24 hours and you can hop on and off the bus as the fancy takes you. **City Sightseeing's** Dublin tour follows a similar route in red open-top double deckers. An audio commentary is available in seven languages. Phone 605 7705 for

59 Upper O'Connell Street. For more detailed service information, telephone 873 4222 or visit their web site at www.dublinbus.ie.

Buses start running from around 6am Monday-Saturday, and 9am on Sundays. Services usually run every 10 to 20 minutes on popular routes although you may have to wait for an hour on some of the quieter routes. Last buses leave the city centre at 11.30pm.

Tickets can be bought on the bus but you will need to have the exact fare ready in coins (notes are not accepted) as most routes operate an autofare system which means that drivers do not have access to cash for security reasons. Deposit your coins into the top of the fare box and, when the driver is satisfied, he will issue you a ticket. If you want to save time and money, however, a range of prepaid tickets can be purchased from Dublin Bus Head Office on Upper O'Connell Street, the Tourist Office on Suffolk Street, and from many newsagents in the greater Dublin area. There are about 270 ticket agents and all have signs outside saying

Dublin Bus Ticket Agent. Prepaid tickets are validated by a machine which you will find to your right as you board the bus. Some of these tickets allow combined access to bus and Luas services, and bus DART and suburban rail services. A selection is outlined below but take note that pre-paid tickets are not valid for travel on Nitelink and City Tours, although Dublin Bus Rambler tickets can be used on Airlink services.

One Day Bus/Rail/Luas Ticket

Unlimited travel for one person by Dublin Bus costs €6; by bus and Luas costs €6.80; by bus DART and suburban rail costs €9.30.

One Day Family Bus Ticket

Unlimited travel for two adults and up to four children under the age of 16 by Dublin Bus costs €10

Three Day Bus Ticket

Unlimited travel for one person by Dublin Bus costs €11.50

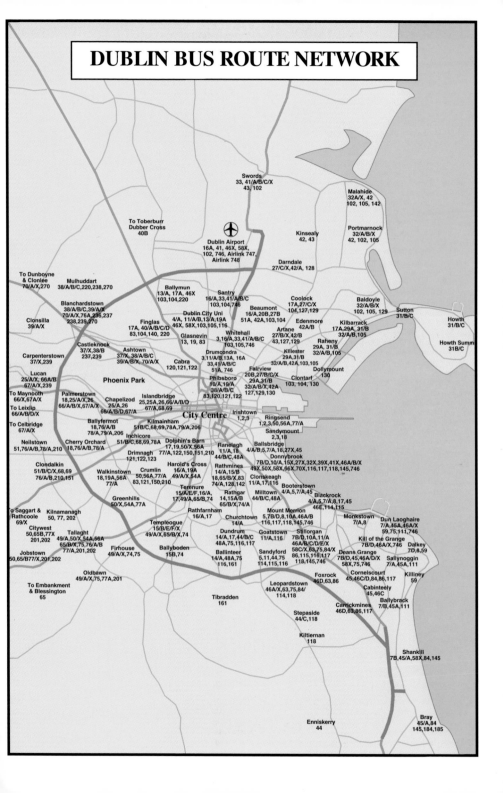

DUBLIN BUS ROUTE NETWORK

more information.

If you want to be that little bit different and see Dublin both by land and water, **Viking Splash Tours** will take you around the city on a Duk, a World War II amphibious vehicle. The tour departs from two locations, Bull Alley beside St Patrick's Cathedral park, and St Stephen's Green North, and winds its way around the city before taking to the waters of the Grand Canal! Departure times and prices vary according to the time of year but there are 10 tours a day during high season when the cost is €20 per adult and €10 for children under 13. The tour lasts for 80 minutes. Tickets are available from departure points or from Dublin Tourism on Suffolk St. Phone 707 6000 for more information.

If you prefer water to land, **Sea Safari** will take you on a one hour tour of Dublin Bay on board one of their high speed inflatables. The itinerary is subject to weather and customer demand, but regularly visited sites include Lambay Island, Ireland's Eye, Bailey Lighthouse, Dalkey Island and Killiney Bay. Departures are from Malahide Marina (phone 806 1626) and from Custom House Quay, opposite Jury's Inn Hotel (phone 855 7600). Cost is €30 per person. Not suitable for kids under eight.

Liffey River Cruises provide a more sedate watertour, leaving and returning to Bachelor's Walk on a 45 minute tour of the Liffey. Cost is €13 per adult. Phone 473 4082 for more information.

Dublin Bus's **Ghostbus Tour** can be good for a laugh as long as you are not spooked by tales of body-snatching and the like. The tour leaves Dublin Bus HQ at 59 Upper O'Connell St, Monday to Friday at 8pm, and 7pm & 9.30pm Saturday to Sunday. The tour lasts 2 hours and costs €25 per adult. Phone 873 4222.

If you would like to see beyond the city, Dublin Bus offers separate tours of the coastline to the north and south of the city. The northern tour lasts for three hours, takes in Malahide Castle and Howth, and costs €25 per adult. The southern tour takes in Powerscourt Estate and the Wicklow Mountains, lasts for 4 hours 30 minutes, and costs €25 per adult. All tours start and finish outside the Dublin Bus HQ at 59 Upper O'Connell Street. Phone 873 4222 for more details.

Bus Eireann runs a good range of sightseeing day tours. Destinations include Newgrange and Kilkenny. Tickets are available from the Tourism Information Centres on Suffolk St and O'Connell St. Phone 836 6111 for further details.

TAXIS

Dublin taxis can be hailed on the street or obtained at one of the many taxi ranks which can be found outside leading hotels, train and bus stations, and at strategic city centre locations such as O'Connell Street, Dame Street, and St Stephen's Green. The good news is that the number of taxis is the road has more than tripled following recent deregulation by Dublin Corporation. The bad news is that queues at taxi ranks can still seem a bit daunting at times, especially late at night when the clubs are closing.

Fares are metered for journeys within 10 miles of the city centre, but there are numerous add-ons for additional passengers, luggage, and unsociable hours. Fares to outlying destinations should be agreed with the driver beforehand, but you should expect to pay about €3 per mile.

CAR HIRE

If you want to explore the country beyond Dublin, a car can be a necessity as the public transport system suffers from severe limitations. Cost is likely to be somewhere between €150 and €300 per week depending on the car, the hire company, and the time of year. See page 62 for a list of hire companies that operate from Dublin Airport. A couple of centrally located offices are listed below:

Hertz `30 F9`
151 South Circular Rd, Dublin 8
Phone 709 3060

Thrifty `25 H7`
26 Lombard St East, Dublin 2
Phone 670 7890

BICYCLE HIRE

Dublin is relatively flat and well suited to exploring by bike, although a good lock and a brave heart in traffic are both very important. Hiring a bike typically costs around €20 per day, or €80 per week.

Cycleways `25 G7`
185 Parnell St, Dublin 1
Phone 873 4748

WALKING TOURS

Of the organised walking tours, the most informative are conducted by history graduates of Trinity College who will take you on a two hour **Historical Walking Tour** of the city and share their considerable knowledge along the way. The tour takes in Trinity College, Old Parliament House, Temple Bar, City Hall, Dublin Castle, Wood Quay, Christ Church Cathedral and the Four Courts.

Tours leave daily from the front gate of Trinity at 11am & 3pm from May to September, daily at 11am during April and October, and at 11am Friday to Sunday during November to March. Cost is €12 per head. Phone 878 0227 for group bookings.

If you like to combine walking with drinking, the **Dublin Literary Pub Crawl** offers a very entertaining tour of some southside pubs associated with Dublin's legion of thirsty writers. The tour starts upstairs at the Duke on Duke Street (see page 82 for times). Phone 670 5602 for information. **The Musical Pub Crawl**, on the other hand, aims to enhance your knowledge of Irish music, starting off upstairs at Oliver St John Gogarty's in Temple Bar. Phone 475 3313. See page 82 for more detail.

Finally, if you would rather conduct your own tour of the city, download an **iWalk** podcast audio guide to your MP3 player free from Dublin Tourism's website at www.visitdublin.com.

The Luas (Irish for speed) runs from city centre to Sandyford and Tallaght

Some would argue that it's due to the free advertising that Ireland used to get when it kept winning the Eurovision Song Contest, but finding a bed when visiting Dublin can be difficult at times, especially at weekends and at any time during the height of the tourist season. For a capital city, Dublin is not over-endowed with hotels, and although more are opening all the time, supply does not always manage to keep up with demand. The golden rule, therefore, is to book your accommodation, either directly or through an agent, before you arrive. A couple of weeks in advance should be enough notice during the quieter times of year, but a month or two might be required if you want to stay in one of the more popular hotels during the summer months.

If you have acted on impulse, however, and find yourself in Dublin with no accommodation booked, reservations can be made at one of the following tourist information centres: Dublin Airport arrivals hall, Dun Laoghaire Ferry Terminal, Suffolk Street and O'Connell Street. Reservations can be made with a credit card by phoning freephone number 1800 363 626 from within Ireland (+353 66 979 2082 from abroad). A deposit is payable at the time of reservation, but this amount is deducted when the final bill is being settled. Touch-screen booking services operate on a 24 hour basis at Dublin Airport, Dun Laoghaire Ferry Terminal, and outside Dublin Tourism Centre on Suffolk Street. Alternatively, reservations can be made by visiting Dublin Tourism's site at www.visitdublin.com.

A small cross section of accommodation is listed below. In an effort to keep things simple, the accommodation has been categorised as 'expensive', 'moderate' or 'budget'. Specific prices are not given as rates often vary according to the time of year and most of the more expensive establishments offer special deals, usually relating to weekend stays. **Laterooms.com** can be a useful source of discounted hotel rooms, especially if you are booking less than a couple of weeks in advance. Some of the city's guest houses offer rather more interesting accommodation than many of the hotels and a couple of the better ones are included in the moderate category.

Family-run B&B's, or townhouses, form the bedrock of budget accommodation, costing around €45 per person sharing, but most are located in the outer suburbs of the city. Premises approved by Failte Ireland normally display a sign to that effect and bookings can be made directly or through the tourist information centres mentioned above. If you are looking for something cheap, but close to the city centre, hostels offer a realistic alternative now that they have shaken off their down-at-heel image. Some have conventional bedrooms but most offer clean and comfortable dorm-style rooms with shared bathrooms. They are inspected and registered by the Tourist Board but are not graded. Price normally depends on how many are sharing, but rates are typically €20-€40 per person per night.

During the summer months, from about mid-June until mid-September, it is possible to book university accommodation at Trinity College and Mercer Court apartments (Royal College of Surgeon's), both of which are right in the heart of the city centre, at UCD to the south of the city centre, and at Dublin City University to the north. Self catering and bed & breakfast accommodation are available and prices start from around €40 per person per night.

All Dublin hotels are assessed by Failte Ireland (the Tourism Development Authority), and each is given a star rating, from one to five stars, to reflect the standard of the accommodation and the facilities available. Guest houses, which tend to be less expensive than hotels, are rated on a similar system, from one to four stars. The appropriate star rating is listed below after the name of each establishment. The hotels and guest houses selected tend to provide rooms with en suite bathroom facilities as standard.

For a more comprehensive list, Dublin Tourism publish an accommodation guide called **Sleep!** which you can purchase from their information centres or via the internet at www.visitdublin.com.

Accommodation Prices

Expensive: Expect to pay in the region of €120 to €200 per night per person sharing, including breakfast.

Moderate: Expect to pay between €50 and €100 per night per person sharing, including breakfast.

Budget: Most budget accommodation costs between €25 and €50 per night per person sharing.

Reservations can be made with a credit card by phoning freephone number 1800 363 626 from within Ireland (+353 66 979 2082 from abroad) or via the internet at www.visitdublin.com

EXPENSIVE

Clarence Hotel***   `25 G7`
6-8 Wellington Quay, Temple Bar
Phone 407 0800. 49 bedrooms
Best known for being owned by Bono and the Edge from the rock band, U2. Controversial redevelopment plans drawn up by Norman Foster have recently been given the green light. If they proceed, the hotel will close temporarily. In the meantime, the hotel restaurant, the **Tea Room** remains highly rated, while the **Octagon Bar** mixes the best cocktails in town. The penthouse suite, with a roof-top hot-tub overlooking the Liffey, is a good place to impress the new woman or man in your life, or simply a good place to put some new life into the one you already have.

The Dylan***   `32 J9`
Eastmoreland Place, Dublin 4
Phone 660 3000. 44 bedrooms
Currently the hippest place to stay in Dublin. Boutique style and a high celebrity quotient.

Four Seasons***   `32 K9`
Simmonscourt Road, Dublin 4
Phone 665 4000. 259 bedrooms
Modern luxury, set within the showgrounds of Dublin's historic RDS. Has quickly established itself at the forefront of the corporate market. Host to many of the city's major social occasions.

Boutique style at the Dylan

Swimming pool and fitness suite.

Merrion Hotel*** `25 H8`
Upper Merrion Street, Dublin 2
Phone 603 0600. 143 bedrooms
Situated across the road from the Irish Parliament, the Merrion started life as four Georgian townhouses. Careful restoration has ensured that the hotel retains much of the charm and elegance of the original buildings, despite extensive modern development to the rear. Swimming pool, gym, and home to Restaurant Patrick Guilbaud, the first restaurant in Ireland to be awarded two Michelin stars.

Shelbourne Hotel*** `25 H8`
27 St Stephen's Green, Dublin 2
Phone 663 4500. 265 bedrooms
The grand old lady of Dublin hotels went under the knife recently but has returned refreshed, but with all her Georgian good looks still intact. Only the very finest, and most expensive, bedrooms get to enjoy the view over St Stephen's Green. Its bustling bars are favourite watering holes for the city's movers and shakers.

Westbury Hotel*** `25 G8`
off Grafton Street, Dublin 2
Phone 679 1122. 205 bedrooms
One of Dublin's leading hotels due primarily to its central but quiet location. An ideal base from which to enjoy the city's shops and nightlife.

MODERATE

Bewley's Hotel* `32 K9`
Merrion Road, Dublin 4

Phone 668 1111 . 304 bedrooms
Former 19th century Masonic School situated close to the RDS in the fashionable suburb of Ballsbridge. All rooms are offered at a fixed rate of € 119, including family rooms which can accommodate two adults and three children.

Central Hotel* `25 G8`
1-5 Exchequer Street, Dublin 2
Phone 679 7302. 70 bedrooms
Central, it is. Ideally located for shopping, and close to the heart of Dublin's thriving nightlife.

Harrington Hall** `25 G8`
69-70 Harcourt Street, Dublin 2
Phone 475 3497. 28 bedrooms
A quiet, Georgian oasis, despite its close proximity to St Stephen's Green and Grafton Street. Personal service, tasteful period decor.

Jurys Inn Christchurch* `25 G8`
Christchurch Place, Dublin 8
Phone 607 0000
182 bedrooms
Jury's Inns spearheaded the move towards charging a flat rate for good value, mid-market, hotel rooms in Dublin. Each room can accommodate up to three adults, or two adults and two children. Other centrally located Jury's Inns can be found north of the river on Custom House Quay and Parnell Street.

Camden Court Hotel* `25 G9`
Camden Street, Dublin 2
Phone 475 9666. 246 bedrooms
Situated a stone's throw from the Luas stop on Harcourt Street, about 5 minutes walk from St Stephen's Green. Excellent facilities include underground car park, Wi-Fi access and leisure and fitness centre with swimming pool.

Number 31 `31 H9`
31 Leeson Close, Dublin 2
Phone 676 5011. 21 Rooms
Hidden jewel. Georgian townhouse offering comfort and personality in a central but very tranquil setting. Breakfasts are legendary.

Premier Suites* `25 H8`
14-17 Lower Leeson Street, Dublin 2
Phone 638 111
Not a cheap option, but if you are looking for stylish self catering accommodation in a prime Georgian location, this could be the solution. Each suite has its own living room and kitchen.

BUDGET

Avalon House `25 G8`
55 Aungier Street, Dublin 2
Phone 475 0001
Well run hostel accommodation for almost 300 guests in single, twin, four and multi-bedded rooms. Convenient location within easy walking distance of St Stephen's Green, Grafton Street and Temple Bar.

Dublin City University `7 H3`
Glasnevin, Dublin 9
Ph 700 5736. 150 rooms, 30 apartments
Single and double en suite bedrooms in modern apartment blocks located about three miles to the north of the city centre. Access to campus facilities which include swimming pool, gym and squash. Early June to early September.

Isaac's Hostel `25 H7`
2-5 Frenchman's Lane, Dublin 1
Phone 855 6215. 22 bedrooms, 28 dorms
Converted wine warehouse which benefits from central location, close to Busaras, Connolly train station and tram stop. Facilities include internet, self-catering kitchen, restaurant, 24 hour reception, pool room and sauna. A tight budget goes a long way here.

Jacob's Inn `25 H7`
21-28 Talbot Place, Dublin 1
Phone 855 5660. 11 bedrooms, 27 dorms
Modern budget accommodation, with excellent facilities right in the heart of the city.

Mercer Court Campus `25 G8`
Lower Mercer Street, Dublin 2
Phone 474 4120. 100 bedrooms
Student accommodation serving the Royal College of Surgeons. Comfortable single and double, en suite rooms, right in the heart of town. Mid-June to mid-September.

Trinity College `25 G7`
College Green, Dublin 2
Phone 896 1177. 589 bedrooms
Not as cheap an option as one might expect, but don't forget that the historic city centre location is factored into the price, and parking is free. Accommodation ranges from rather monastic single rooms which overlook the cobbles and cost around €50, to modern self catering apartments on the edge of campus. Mid-June to late September.

Abbey Theatre
See page 76.

Bank of Ireland `25 G7`
2 College Green, Dublin 2
Phone 677 6801
One of Dublin's most impressive buildings, the Bank of Ireland began life as Parliament House in 1729 but, when the Act of Union was passed in 1800, the government of Ireland was transferred to London, and the building was later sold and converted into a bank. The main banking hall now occupies what was once the House of Commons chamber but the House of Lords chamber has survived in tact. Items of interest include the parliamentary mace, an impressive Waterford crystal chandelier dating from 1765, and two large 18th century tapestries depicting the Battle of the Boyne in 1690 and the Siege of Derry in 1689. The building can be visited free of charge from Monday to Friday during banking hours, and there are guided tours of the House of Lords.

Beaches
The suburban rail system and the DART put quite a few sandy beaches within easy reach of the city centre. These include Portmarnock and Balbriggan to the north and Killiney to the south.

Casino at Marino `18 K4`
Cherrymount Crescent, Dublin 3
Phone 833 1618
Not a casino, as we know it, but an architectural gem built in the 1760's as a pleasure house for the Earl of Charlemont in the grounds of Marino Estate. Marino House was demolished in 1920 and much of the estate was sold off for development. Fortunately, the Casino, which actually means "small house", survives as a glorious folly. Guided tours of the building are conducted daily from 10am-6pm between June and September; 10am-5pm daily during May & October; Feb/March/Apr/Nov, Sat & Sun 12noon-4pm. Closed December & January Admission charge is €2.90 per adult.

Chester Beatty Library
See page 74.

Chimney Viewing Tower `24 F7`
Smithfield Village, Dublin 7
Phone 817 3838
Panoramic views of Dublin available from a glass enclosed observation platform perched on top of the old Jameson distillery chimney. A glass walled lift

Trinity College - a tranquil oasis right in the heart of the city

takes you 220 feet above ground. *At the time of writing, the tower is closed for essential maintenance.*

Christ Church Cathedral `25 G8`
Christchurch Place, Dublin 8
Phone 677 8099
The Cathedral of the Holy Trinity, or Christ Church as it is commonly known, is one of two Church of Ireland cathedrals in Dublin and the city's oldest building with sections dating back to 1172. The cathedral was founded by Sitric, the Norse King of Dublin, in 1030 but it was the Normans, led by Strongbow, who rebuilt the original wooden structure in stone. Much of the building collapsed due to subsidence in 1562 and most of what is seen above ground today is the result of major restoration work carried out during the 19th century. The vast crypt, which dates back to the Norman period, houses the Treasures of Christ Church exhibition. Services at least 3 times a day (all denominations welcome). Choral Evensong takes place at 6pm on Wednesdays and Thursdays, 5pm on Saturdays (except July & August), and 3.30pm on Sundays. *Opening Times: Mon-Sun 10am-5pm. Admission charge is €6 per adult.*

City Hall `25 G8`
Dame Street, Dublin 2
Phone 222 2204
Completed in 1779 as the Royal Exchange, the building became the centre of municipal government in 1852. The City Hall's most striking feature is its interior rotunda with a central mosaic depicting the city's coat of arms, and

a series of frescos depicting the heraldic arms of the four Irish provinces and various aspects of Dublin. A multimedia exhibition entitled 'The Story of the Capital' traces the history of the city over the past 1,000 years. Admission is €4 per adult. Tours of the city hall are also available. *Opening Times: Mon-Sat 10am-5.15pm, Sun 2pm-5pm.*

Custom House `25 H7`
Custom House Quay, Dublin 1
Phone 888 2538
One of Dublin's finest Georgian buildings, Custom House has been a familiar part of the city skyline since it was completed in 1791. Designed by James Gandon, who was also responsible for the Four Courts, the building's classical facade is built from Portland stone and is best viewed from across the river. The rooftop statues of Neptune, Mercury, Plenty and Industry represent various aspects of transport and trade, and the statue on top of the central copper dome represents Hope. Although the building was ravaged by fire during the War of Independence in 1921, it was later restored. A visitor centre is located in and around the dome area of the building. Admission is €1 per adult. *Opening Times: Mid March-Oct, Mon-Fri 10am-12.30pm, Sat-Sun 2pm-5pm; Nov- mid March, Wed-Fri 10am-12.30pm, Sun 2pm-5pm*

Dalkey Castle & Heritage Centre
Castle St, Dalkey, Co. Dublin
Phone 285 8366
Restored 15th century castle housing a heritage centre which outlines the history of Dalkey, the surrounding area, and

Custom House reflected in the waters of the River Liffey

its many literary associations (the 2nd chapter of Joyce's *Ulysses* is set in Dalkey), as well as providing exhibition space for Irish art and crafts. *Opening Times: Mon-Fri 9.30am-5pm, Sat & Sun 11am-5pm. Admission charge is €6 per adult.*

The Douglas Hyde Gallery `25 H8`
Trinity College, Dublin 2
(Nassau Street entrance)
Phone 896 1116
Arts Council backing has helped to convert this rather minimalist space into one of Ireland's leading contemporary art galleries, hosting a busy programme of exhibitions by emerging and well-established artists from home and abroad. *Opening Times: Mon- Fri 11am-6pm (Thurs until 7pm), Sat 11am-4.45pm*

Dublin Castle `25 G7`
Dame Street, Dublin 2
Phone 645 8813
Large parts of Dublin Castle have been rebuilt over the centuries and the building today is more palatial in style than one might expect. The original castle was built on the orders of King John in 1204 on the site of an earlier Viking fortification, remnants of which have been preserved and are on view at the 'Undercroft'. Dublin Castle was at the heart of British military and administrative rule in Ireland for 700 years and it was used during that time as a military fortress, a prison, record office, courts of law and residence of the British viceroys of Ireland. The fact that the statue of Justice above the main gate stands with her back turned towards the

city was seen by Dubliners as an apt symbol of British rule. Presidents of Ireland are now inaugurated in the castle and its facilities are used to host European Union conferences and summits. The castle's State Apartments, Undercroft and Chapel Royal are open to visitors. *Opening Times: Mon-Fri 10am-4.45pm, Sat-Sun 2pm-4.45pm. Admission charge is €4.50 per adult..*

Dublin City Gallery The Hugh Lane
See page 74.

Dublin Tourism Centre `25 G8`
Suffolk Street, Dublin 2
www.visitdublin.com
Phone 1850 230 330 from Ireland
Phone 0800 039 7000 from UK
Impressive premises housed in the former church of St Andrew. Services include tourist information and accommodation reservations for the whole of Ireland, a bookstore, gift shop, café, bureau de change, and booking facilities for theatres, bus and rail tours. Other tourism offices can be found on Upper O'Connell Street, at Dublin Airport arrivals hall, and at Dun Laoghaire ferry terminal. *Opening hours at Suffolk Street are Mon-Sat 9pm-5.30pm (until 7pm June-September), Sun 10.30pm-3pm (until 5pm July & August).*

Dublin Writers Museum
See page 74.

Dublin Zoo `15 D6`
Phoenix Park, Dublin 8
Phone 474 8900
The Zoo was founded in 1830 making it

the third oldest in the world. It is situated in the Phoenix Park, within easy reach of the main entrance on Parkgate Street. The Zoo places a heavy emphasis on the breeding of endangered species, but there is plenty to see, including a daily feeding programme for gorillas, polar bears, reptiles, sea-lions and elephants. Areas include World of Cats, World of Primates, Fringes of the Arctic, and a new 30 acre extension to the Zoo called African Plains, with rhinos, hippos, lions, cheetahs, chimpanzees and giraffes among the residents. *Opening Times: Mon-Sat 9.30am-6.30pm (until dusk during winter); Sun 10.30am-6.30pm. Admission is €14.50 per adult, €10 per child, free for kids under 3*

Dublinia & Viking World `25 G8`
St Michael's Hill,
Christchurch, Dublin 8
Phone 679 4611
The story of medieval Dublin using reconstructed streets and houses, and an array of citizens of the time. *Opening Times: April-Sept, Mon-Sun 10am-5pm; Oct-March, Mon-Sat 11am-4pm, Sunday 10.00am-4pm. Admission is €6.25 per adult.*

Four Courts `24 F7`
Inns Quay, Dublin 7
Home to the Irish law courts since 1796, the Four Courts building has much in common with Custom House. Both were designed by James Gandon and both required major restoration following fire damage suffered during the turbulence of 1921 and 1922. The public is admitted only when the courts are in session.

Fry Model Railway Museum
See page 74.

GAA Museum
See page 74.

Gallery of Photography `25 G7`
Meeting House Square, Temple Bar
Phone 671 4654
Ireland's only gallery devoted exclusively to photography plays host to both Irish and international exhibitions, which are accompanied by talks and workshops. Services available include restoring and copying old photographs. *Opening Times: Tues-Sat 11am-6pm; Sun 1pm-6pm. Admission is free.*

General Post Office `25 G7`
O'Connell Street, Dublin 1
Phone 705 7000
The General Post Office was built in

1815 and is best known for its role as rebel headquarters during the 1916 Easter Rising. All but destroyed in the ensuing battle, it re-opened in 1929 and continues in public use today. *Open Mon-Sat 8am-8pm. Admission is free.*

Grafton Street `25 G8`
Grafton Street is Dublin's premier shopping street (see page 80). Even if you suffer from a retail allergy, it is worth taking a leisurely stroll along this pedestrianised thoroughfare to enjoy its array of street theatre, talented buskers, and other colourful characters.

Guinness Storehouse `24 F7`
St James's Gate, Dublin 8
Phone 408 4800
www.guinness-storehouse.com
All you ever wanted to know about the 250 year history of the 'black stuff', from the brewing process through to the iconic advertising and merchandising of the product. Exhibition space covers seven floors of an impressive visitor centre, and the tour finishes with a complimentary pint and panoramic views of the city from the Gravity Bar, which occupies the top floor of the building. Ireland's most popular tourist attraction drawing nearly one million visitors annually. Admission is €14 per adult. Avoid queues and receive a 10% discount by booking online. *Opening Times: Mon-Sun 9.30am-5pm (until 7pm July & August).*

Halfpenny Bridge `25 G7`
Bachelor's Walk
The Ha'penny Bridge is a cast-iron footbridge which spans the Liffey, providing a convenient gateway to Temple Bar if you are crossing from the north side of the river. Built in 1816, the halfpenny toll no longer applies today!

Howth `13 V2`
If you are only in Dublin for a couple of days, and don't have time to make it out to the west of Ireland, take a trip to Howth instead. Only a twenty minute DART ride north of the city centre, this beautiful fishing village is a world away from the hustle and bustle of downtown Dublin. Great seascapes and coastal walks, and some good bars and restaurants (see pages 82-96).

Irish Film Centre
See page 77.

Irish Jewish Museum
See page 74.

Irish Museum of Modern Art

See page 74.

James Joyce Centre
See page 74.

James Joyce Museum
See page 75.

Kilmainham Gaol `23 D8`
Inchicore Road, Kilmainham, D8
Phone 453 5984
The jail opened in 1796 but has not held any prisoners since 1924. Today it is a museum to the countless Irish patriots who were imprisoned here from 1798 until the release of the last inmate, Eamon de Valera, who went on to become Prime Minister, then President of Ireland. The darkest episode in the gaol's history was the execution of Patrick Pearse, James Connolly and 14 other leaders of the 1916 Easter Rising. A guided tour of the jail includes an audio-visual presentation and various exhibits relating to the struggle for Irish independence. The gaol has been used many times as a film location, including an appearance in the *Italian Job*. *Opening Times: Apr-Sept, Mon-Sun 9.30am-5pm; Oct-Mar, Mon-Sat 9.30am-4pm, Sun 10am-5pm. Admission is €5.30 per adult.*

Leinster House `25 H8`
Kildare Street, Dublin 2
Leinster House is the seat of Irish government; home to Dáil Eireann (House of Representatives) which comprises 166 elected TD's, and Seanad Eireann (Senate) to which 60 senators are appointed. Erected in 1745, the building is only open to the public when parliament is not sitting.

Malahide Castle
Malahide, County Dublin
Phone 846 2184
This charming castle has been both a fortress and the family home of the Talbots for nearly 800 years, right up until the last Lord Talbot died in 1973. The architecture reflects many different styles, and the interior is enhanced by an impressive collection of period fur-

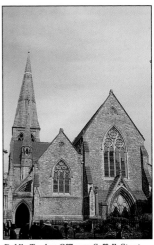

Dublin Tourism Office on Suffolk Street

niture and a series of historic Irish portraits, most of which are on loan from the National Gallery. The castle stands in 250 acres of park land which is also open to the public. *Opening Times: Mon-Sat 10am-5pm, Sun 10am-6pm. Admission charge is €7.25 per adult.*

Mansion House `25 H8`
Dawson Street, Dublin 2
The Mansion House has been the official residence of the Lord Mayor of Dublin since 1715. The first Irish Parliament met here in 1919 to adopt Ireland's Declaration of Independence. The house is not open to the public.

Marsh's Library
See page 75.

Merrion Square `25 H8`
The best preserved Georgian square in Dublin and, as the wall plaques indicate, home to many historic figures including Daniel O'Connell, W. B. Yeats and Oscar Wilde. A statue of Wilde overlooks his old home - Dubliners refer to it as the 'fag on the crag'. The public gardens in the centre of the square are a hidden gem and well worth a stroll on a sunny afternoon.

National Botanic Gardens `16 F4`
Glasnevin, Dublin 9
Phone 804 0300
The Gardens were founded by the Royal Dublin Society in 1795 and contain some 20,000 species of trees, plants and shrubs, many housed within Victorian curvilinear glasshouses. *Opening Times: Mid Feb-Mid Nov, daily 9am-6pm; Mid Nov-Mid Feb,*

5 For Kids

Dublin Zoo
Viking Splash (see p66)
Dublinia
Sea Safari (see p66)
Newbridge House & Farm

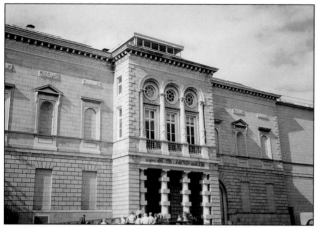

The National Gallery of Ireland - one of the leading state galleries in Europe

daily 9am-4.30pm. Admission is free.

National Concert Hall
See page 77.

National Gallery of Ireland
See page 75.

National Library of Ireland
See page 75.

National Museum of Ireland-Archaeology
See page 75.

National Museum of Ireland-Decorative Arts & History
See page 75.

National Museum of Ireland-Natural History
See page 75.

National Photographic Archive
See page 75.

National Print Museum
See page 75.

National Transport Museum
See page 75.

Newbridge House & Farm
Donabate, Co. Dublin
Phone 843 6534
Magnificent manor, built for the Archbishop of Dublin in 1740. The house stands in 350 acres of parkland and boasts one of the finest Georgian interiors in Ireland. There is much of interest outside as well as in, including a dairy, a blacksmith's forge and a 29 acre traditional farm, complete with farmyard animals. *Opening Times: April-Sept, Tues-Sat 10am-5pm, Sun 2pm-6pm; Oct-March, Sat & Sun 2pm-5pm. Admission charge is €6.50 per adult.*

Newman House `25 H8`
85-86 St Stephen's Green, Dublin 2
Phone 716 7422
Cardinal Newman founded a Catholic University here in the mid-19th century and former scholars include the poet Gerard Manley Hopkins and James Joyce. The building has some of the finest Georgian interiors to be seen anywhere in Dublin. *Opening Times: June-Aug, Tues-Fri, tours at 2pm, 3pm and 4pm Admission cost is €5 per adult.*

Number Twenty Nine `25 H8`
29 Fitzwilliam Street Lower, Dublin 2
Phone 702 6165
Fitzwilliam Street epitomises Georgian Dublin and the idea behind number 29 is to convey what it was like (from the inside) to live as a middle class Dublin family in the early 1800's. The house has been preserved by the Electricity Supply Board in an act of contrition for tearing down most of the rest of the street to build an ugly 1960's office block. *Opening Times: Tues-Sat 10am-5pm, Sun 1pm-5pm. Admission charge is €6 per adult.*

Old Jameson Distillery `24 F7`
Bow Street, Smithfield, Dublin 7
Phone 807 2355
The Old Jameson Distillery guides you through the ancient craft of whiskey making with the help of an audio-visual presentation, a museum and, of course, the Jameson bar where you can sample

a drop or two of the 'water of life'. *Opening Times: Mon-Sun 9am-6pm (last tour 5.30pm). Admission charge is €11 per adult.*

Phoenix Park `23 D7`
The Phoenix Park is one of the largest city parks in Europe, covering 1760 acres and surrounded by a wall which is 8 miles long. The park is predominantly open grassland, grazed by a herd of deer, but it has a few notable residents including the Irish President who lives at Aras an Uachtaráin, and the US Ambassador. The main visitor attraction is Dublin Zoo (see page 70), but another place of interest is the Phoenix Park Visitor Centre which is in the grounds of the old Papal Nunciature, near to the Phoenix monument (use Ashtown Gate, admission is free). For something a little bit different, catch a game of polo in the park from May to September. The main entrance to the park is on Parkgate Street.

Royal Hibernian Academy
See page 75.

St Audoen's Church `25 G8`
High Street, Dublin 8
Phone 677 0088
The only remaining medieval parish church in Dublin, dedicated to St Ouen, the 7th century bishop of Rouen, patron saint of Normandy. *Opening Times: May-Oct daily 9.30am-5.30pm*

St Mary's Pro Cathedral `25 G7`
Marlborough Street, Dublin 1
Phone 874 5441
Despite the predominance of Catholicism, Dublin has not had a Catholic cathedral since the Reformation, and so worshippers have had to rely on 'the pro' since 1825. Built in Greek classical style, plans to build a grander cathedral on Merrion Square were thankfully abandoned even though the Church acquired the land back in the 1920's. A good time to visit is Sunday at 11am when Latin Mass is sung by the Palistrina Choir.

St Michan's Church `24 F7`
Church Street Lower, Dublin 7
Phone 872 4154
The church houses an organ which is thought to have been played by Handel, but the main attraction is the mummified bodies which can be viewed in the crypt! Guided tours, Mon-Sat, €4 per adult.

St Patrick's Cathedral `25 G8`
St Patrick's Close, Dublin 8

Phone 475 4817

Like Christ Church, St Patrick's is a Church of Ireland cathedral with an ancient and chequered history. The current building dates back to 1191 but a church has stood on this site since 450 A.D., marking the fact that Saint Patrick used a well within the cathedral grounds to baptise converts into the Christian faith. The cathedral was ravaged by fires and storms during the 14th century and its appearance today owes much to 19th century restoration work paid for by the Guinness family. Jonathan Swift, author of *Gulliver's Travels*, was Dean of St Patrick's from 1713 to 1747, and he is buried within its walls. The cathedral's choir school was established in 1432 and its choristers gave the first performance of Handel's *Messiah* back in 1742. *Opening Times: Mon-Sun 9am-6pm. Admission charge is €5.50 per adult. Closed to visitors 30 minutes before services.*

St Stephen's Green `25 H8`

As soon as they glimpse the summer sun, many Dubliners head straight for the natural delights of St Stephen's Green. This urban oasis was originally a piece of common land used for public hangings among other things but, by 1880, it had become a public garden thanks to the benevolence of Lord Ardilaun, a member of the Guinness family. Lunchtime concerts in the summer months.

Shaw's Birthplace `31 G9`

33 Synge St, Dublin 8

Phone 475 0854

Life for George Bernard Shaw, playwright and Nobel Prize winner, began in 1856 at this Victorian terrace, and the interior has been restored to reflect life at that time. *Opening Times: May-Sept, Mon-Tues & Thurs-Fri, 10am-5pm, Sat-Sun 2am-5pm. Admission charge is €7.25 per adult.*

The Spire of Dublin `25 G7`

A millennium project, known locally as 'the spike' or 'the stiletto in the ghetto', the stainless steel spire forms a focal point for the redevelopment of O'Connell St. At 120 metres in height, it stands in a place formerly occupied by Lord Nelson until he was blown off his column by the IRA in 1966, to mark the 50th anniversary of the Easter Rising.

Temple Bar `25 G7`

The Temple Bar area is sandwiched between Dame Street and the River Liffey, with Westmoreland Street to the east and Fishamble Street to the west acting as its other boundaries. This is one of the oldest areas of Dublin, but it had been in decline for many years when plans were made in the 1980's to redevelop a large part of it as a bus station. Enter Irish Taoiseach (Prime Minister), Charles Haughey, who decided that Temple Bar should become the beneficiary of several major cultural projects. Like President Miterrand of France, Mr Haughey hoped that his lasting legacy would be to the Arts although, as things turned out, most Dubliners remember him for his ability to attract large financial gifts. Temple Bar, as it happens, is often described as Dublin's Left Bank. The area, which is characterised by its narrow cobbled streets, is now peppered with galleries, design studios, theatres, cinemas, cultural centres, alternative shops and many good pubs, clubs and restaurants. Meeting House Square is home to **Temple Bar Outdoors,** a year-round programme of free, outdoor cultural activity which includes live performances, film screenings and family events. **The Temple Bar Food Market** also sets up in Meeting House Square, every Saturday 10am-5pm. Other regular events include a Saturday book market on Temple Bar Square, and a chance to climb onto your soap box come Sunday afternoon at **Speakers' Square**, also on Temple Bar Square. On the downside, the success of the area has attracted a lot of stag and hen parties, and celebrations have been known to get out of hand occasionally. Many businesses have recently responded by banning stag groups from pubs and clubs in Temple Bar. For more information on what's on in the area visit the **Temple Bar Cultural Information Centre** on East Essex Street or go to www.templebar.ie

Trinity College & The Book of Kells

College Street, Dublin 2

Phone 896 2320 `25 G7`

Founded in 1592 by Queen Elizabeth I using land confiscated from the Priory

The Hugh Lane Gallery

Joyce admiring the 'stiletto in the ghetto'

of All Hallows, Trinity College is the oldest university in Ireland. Despite its city centre location, the 40 acre campus is a tranquil world containing an impressive array of buildings dating from the 17th to the 20th century. The college has had an uneasy relationship with the Catholic Church, and it was not until the death of Archbishop McQuaid in 1970 that the Church lifted its boycott and proclaimed that it was no longer a mortal sin for a Catholic to attend Trinity. The college displays many treasures, the best known being the **Book of Kells**, a 9th century illustrated manuscript of the Gospels, often described as 'the most beautiful book in the world'. Other visitor attractions include the Douglas Hyde Gallery, which specialises in contemporary art. There is free public access to the College and it is well worth a visit just to sample the rarefied atmosphere of its cobbled squares and college greens. There is an admission charge of €8 per adult to see the Old Library which houses the Book of Kells. *The Old Library is open Mon-Sat 9.30am-5pm, Sun 12noon-4.30pm.*

Whitefriar Street Carmelite Church

56 Aungier Street, Dublin 2

Phone 475 8821 `25 G8`

The church stands on the site of a Carmelite Priory which was founded in 1278, but the current building was not started until 1825. The church contains several interesting relics donated by Pope Gregory XVI in 1835, the best known being the remains of St Valentine.

The list that follows is certainly not an exhaustive one - Dublin has an array of small galleries dotted around the city, especially in the Temple Bar district. The admission prices listed are based on one adult, but concessions are normally available for children and groups, and sometimes for students and the unemployed. For more detailed information, simply phone the appropriate number given below.

Chester Beatty Library `25 G7`
Dublin Castle, Dame St, Dublin 2
Phone 407 0750
European Museum of the Year 2002, and a must-see attraction. The library, which overlooks Dubh Linn Garden, a tranquil oasis in the grounds of Dublin Castle, houses a collection of 22,000 items bequeathed to the nation by Sir Alfred Chester Beatty in 1968, including a treasure trove of Islamic manuscripts, Chinese, Japanese, Indian and other Oriental art. Biblical papyri, other early Christian manuscripts, Western prints and printed books complete one of the richest collections of its kind in the world. A spiritual place. *Opening Times: Mon-Fri 10am-5pm (closed Mondays Oct-Apr), Sat 11am-5pm, Sun 1pm-5pm. Admission is free.*

Dublin City Gallery `17 G6`
The Hugh Lane
Parnell Square North, Dublin 1
Phone 222 5550
Situated in Charlemont House, a magnificent 18th century townhouse, the gallery is named after Hugh Lane, an Irish art lover who bequeathed many major works to the gallery after his death in the 1915 sinking of the Lusitania. French Impressionists are well represented with works by Manet, Monet, Degas and Renoir, and there is also a large collection of 20th century Irish art including paintings by J B Yeats and stained glass panels by Harry Clarke. In 2001 the gallery acquired the studio of Francis Bacon and its entire contents, numbering 7,500 items. The studio has been faithfully reconstructed as a permanent exhibit. The gallery added 2,000 square metres of exhibition space in 2006 and the new extension

includes the Sean Scully Room, housing 8 paintings donated by the artist. Free concerts and lectures on Sundays. *Opening Times: Tues-Thurs 10am-6pm, Fri & Sat 10am-5pm, Sun 11am-5pm. Admission is free to the permanent collection.*

Dublin Writers Museum `17 G6`
18 Parnell Square North, Dublin 1
Phone 872 2077
Housed in a beautifully restored 18th century mansion, the Writers Museum opened in 1991 to mark the great literary tradition which Dublin has cultivated over the past 300 years. On display are letters, first editions, portraits and other personal items belonging to a galaxy of Irish writers including Joyce, Shaw, Beckett, Wilde, Yeats, Swift, Sheridan, O'Casey and Behan. The museum hosts exhibitions and readings and has a special room devoted to children's literature. *Opening Times: Mon-Sat 10am-5pm, Sun 11am-5pm. Late opening until 6pm Mon-Fri during June, July & August. Admission charge is €7.25 per adult.*

Fry Model Railway Museum
Malahide Castle Demesne,
Malahide
Phone 846 3779
Impressive model railway layout which recreates much of Ireland's transport system in miniature, complemented by separate displays of hand crafted railway models and other memorabilia. *Opening Times: April-Sept, Mon-Thurs & Sat 10am-5pm, Sun 1pm-5pm. Admission price is €7.25 per adult.*

GAA Museum/Croke Park `17 H5`
St Joseph's Avenue, Dublin 3
Phone 819 2323
The museum charts the history of the Gaelic Athletic Association since it was founded in 1884. Displays include trophies and artefacts from the games of gaelic football and hurling, with audio visual and touchscreen technology on hand to help recall famous games and players from past and present. Interactive technology allows you to test your sporting skills. See where the action actually takes place with a tour of the stadium, which is Europe's 4th largest arena with a capacity of more than 80,000.

Opening Times: Mon-Sat 9.30am-5pm, Sun 12noon-5pm. Admission charge is €5.50 per adult for the museum, €10.50 to include stadium tour.

Irish Jewish Museum
3-4 Walworth Rd, Dublin 8 `31 G9`
Phone 490 1857
The museum, which is housed in a former synagogue, chronicles the history of Jews in Ireland. *Opening Times: May-Sept, Tues/Thurs/Sun 11am-3.30pm; Oct-April, Sun 10.30am-2.30pm. Admission is free.*

Irish Museum of Modern Art
Royal Hospital, Military Road, Kilmainham, Dublin 8
Phone 612 9900 `24 E8`
Modelled on *Les Invalides* in Paris, the Royal Hospital was built in 1684, not as a hospital, but as a home for retired soldiers and it remained so until the 20th century. One of the finest buildings in Ireland, it was restored in 1986 and opened as a museum in 1991. Its permanent collection, together with temporary exhibitions, provide a showcase for Irish and international art mainly from the second half of the 20th century. *Opening Times: Tues-Sat 10am-5.30pm, Sun 12noon-5.30pm. Admission is free.*

James Joyce Centre
35 Nth Great George's St, `17 G6`
Dublin 1
Phone 878 8547
The James Joyce Centre is housed in a beautifully restored 18th century Georgian townhouse which, although associated with Joyce, was never actually his home. The centre promotes the life and work of Joyce with daily talks, conducted tours of the house, and a walking tour through the Joyce country of north Dublin. Facilities include a coffee shop and bookshop, and visitors are welcome to use the reference library. *Opening Times: Tues-Sat 10am-5pm. Admission to the house is €5 per adult. Walking tour €10.*

James Joyce Museum
Joyce Tower, Sandycove
Phone 280 9265
The museum is housed in a Martello tower where Joyce stayed for a week in 1904 as the guest of Oliver St John Gogarty who inspired the

author to create the unsavoury character, Buck Mulligan. Much of the first chapter of *Ulysses* is actually set in the tower. Exhibits include letters, books, photographs and personal possessions of Joyce. *Opening Times: Apr-Sept, Mon-Sat 10am-5pm, Sun 2pm-6pm. Admission charge is €7.25 per adult.*

Marsh's Library `25 G8`
St Patrick's Close, Dublin 8
Phone 454 3511
Built in 1701 by Archbishop Narcissus Marsh, this is the oldest public library in Ireland. It was designed by Sir William Robinson who was also the architect for the Royal Hospital, Kilmainham. The library contains 25,000 books and manuscripts, most dating from the 16th to the 18th centuries. The interior is dominated by carved oak and includes three wired alcoves or 'cages' where scholars were once locked in while they studied rare volumes. *Opening Times: Mon/Wed-Fri 10am-1pm & 2pm-5pm; Sat 10.30am-1pm. Admission charge is €2.50 per adult, children free.*

National Gallery of Ireland
Merrion Square West, Dublin 2
Phone 661 5133 `25 H8`
The National Gallery of Ireland first opened in 1864 but by the late 1980's it had fallen on hard times, so much so that one art-lover was able to remove a small French oil and post it back to the gallery in protest at the state of disrepair and lack of security. How times have changed. The Gallery has undergone major refurbishment which has seen the opening of a Yeats Museum, and a new 4,000 square metre extension, the Millennium Wing, which has its own entrance on Clare Street. It now ranks among the leading state galleries in Europe, attracting over one million visitors a year to view a collection which includes work by Rembrandt, Titian, Goya, El Greco, Monet, Degas and Picasso. There are free guided tours at 3pm on Saturdays, and on Sundays at 2pm, 3pm and 4pm. *Opening Times: Mon-Sat 9.30am-5.30pm (until 8.30pm Thurs), Sun 12noon-5.30pm. Admission is free to the permanent collection.*

National Library of Ireland
Kildare Street, Dublin 2 `25 H8`
Phone 603 0200
With over half a million volumes and an historic collection of Irish newspapers, photographs, maps and prints, this is the country's leading library for Irish studies. You will need a reader's ticket, which can be obtained free of charge, to enjoy the Reading Room with its stately dome. The library's **Genealogy Advisory Service** is invaluable to those looking to research their family history in Ireland. *Opening Times: Mon-Wed 9.30am-9pm; Thurs-Fri 9.30am-5pm; Sat 9.30am-1pm. Admission is free.*

National Museum of Ireland-
Archaeology `25 H8`
Kildare Street, Dublin 2
Phone 677 7444
Opened in 1890, the National Museum contains a magnificent collection of Irish treasures and artefacts dating from the Stone Age to the 20th century. The Centrecourt houses 'Or - Ireland's Gold' exhibition featuring jewellery and metal work dating from the Bronze Age, 2,000 years ago. The Treasury displays the Ardagh Chalice, Tara Brooch, Cross of Cong and many other examples of outstanding medieval Celtic craftsmanship, accompanied by an audio-visual programme explaining their archaeological background. Other displays include Viking Age Ireland, Medieval Ireland 1150-1550, and Kingship & Sacrifice which exhibits a number of recently discovered bog bodies dating back to the Iron Age. *Opening Times: Tues-Sat 10am-5pm, Sun 2pm-5pm. Admission is free. Tours available at €2 per person.*

National Museum of Ireland-
Decorative Arts and History
Collins Barracks, Benburb St, Dublin 7 `24 F7`
Phone 677 7444
The oldest military barracks in Europe is now home to the National Museum's collection of decorative arts and artefacts relating to the economic, social, political and military history of the state. Displays include silver work, ceramics, glass, period furniture, weaponry, scientific instruments and textiles. *Opening Times: Tues-Sat 10am-5pm, Sun 2pm-5pm. Admission is free.*

National Museum of Ireland-
Natural History `25 G8`
Merrion Street, Dublin 2
Phone 677 7444
Currently closed for refurbishment.

National Photographic Archive
Meeting House Square, `25 G7`
Temple Bar, Dublin 2.
Phone 603 0374
A new, purpose-built offshoot of the National Library, housing more than 600,000 photographs, as well as exhibition space and a reading room. *Opening Times: Mon-Fri 10am-5pm, Sat 10am-2pm (exhibition area only). Admission is free.*

National Print Museum `26 J8`
Garrison Chapel, Beggars Bush, Haddington Road, Dublin 4
Phone 660 3770
Museum dedicated to the preservation of the machinery and printing techniques employed before the advent of computers. *Opening Times: Mon-Fri 9am-5pm, Sat-Sun 2pm-5pm. Admission charge is €3.50 per adult.*

National Transport Museum
Howth Castle Demesne, Howth
Phone 848 0831 `13 U2`
The museum is run by a group of volunteers dedicated to the preservation of Ireland's transport heritage. Exhibits include old buses, trams, fire engines and military vehicles. *Opening Times: June-August, Mon-Fri 10am-5pm, Sat-Sun 2pm-5pm; Sept-May Sat-Sun 2pm-5pm. Admission charge is €3 per adult, €1.50 per child.*

Royal Hibernian Academy `25 H8`
15 Ely Place, Dublin 2
Phone 661 2558
Large, modern gallery space dedicated to exhibitions of Irish and international art while affording an opportunity for artists without commercial representation in Dublin to test their commercial viability. At the time of writing, the gallery is due to reopen after a lengthy period of refurbishment work. *Opening Times: Tues-Wed/Fri-Sat 11am-5pm, Thurs 11am-8pm, Sun 2pm-5pm. Admission is free.*

If you are planning an evening out at the theatre, cinema or a performance of live music or comedy, it's a good idea to pick up a free copy of *The Event Guide* which is published fortnightly and distributed through shops, cafés and bars around the city. It provides an excellent and comprehensive guide to what's on, including a series of current reviews. If you are on-line, try www.entertainment.ie for another source of up to date reviews and listings.

THEATRE

For a city steeped in literary tradition, it is only fitting that the Dublin theatre scene is a vibrant one. The Abbey is the most famous theatre in town, premiering the work of many Irish playwrights (see below). It occupies the mainstream along with the Gate and the Gaiety, but variety abounds, with theatres such as the Peacock and the Project staging many works of a more experimental nature. And with fresh writing talent such as Frank McGuinness, Martin McDonagh and Conor McPherson, Irish theatre goers are able to enjoy a good selection of contemporary drama as well as the catalogue of better known work from the past.

Dublin theatre is very accessible and need not be expensive. The drama society of Trinity College, Dublin University Players, may be an amateur company but their output is often of a high standard and they give regular performances from October through to April, some at lunchtime. The prices are very cheap and the Players Theatre, part of the Samuel Beckett Theatre, is convenient to the city centre.

The highlight of the theatrical calendar is the Dublin Theatre Festival and its Fringe. The main festival runs for two weeks in late September and early October, while the fringe runs for a couple of weeks beforehand. The theatre festival has been running for longer than the Edinburgh Festival and, like its Scottish counterpart, it manages to attract performers from the four corners of the globe. For more information, visit www.dublintheatrefestival.com. The fringe festival focuses primarily on the lighter side of life and includes a wide variety of comedy, cabaret, dance and musical performances, staged at a multitude of smaller venues across the city, including many pubs. For more information visit www.fringefest.com.

Finally, when booking theatre tickets over the phone, it might be useful to refer to the seating plans published in the theatre section of the Golden Pages telephone directory.

Abbey Theatre `25 H7`
26 Lower Abbey Street, Dublin 1
Phone 878 7222 (Box Office)
The Abbey and the Peacock, which share the same site, are the two theatres of the National Theatre which was founded in 1904 by Nobel Laureate, William Butler Yeats, and Lady Gregory. The original theatre was destroyed by fire in 1951 which explains the rather uninspiring 1960's replacement which is due, in turn, to be replaced by a new building surrounded by water on George's Dock between the IFSC and the CHQ building. The Abbey promotes new Irish writing and, to this end, it has premiered the work of every leading Irish playwright over the past century, including Sean O'Casey, J. M. Synge, Brian Friel and Frank McGuinness. It has also unearthed a rich seam of acting talent such as Barry Fitzgerald, Ray McAnally and Cyril Cusack. The theatre has earned a well deserved international reputation for the quality of its productions which also include the work of playwrights from beyond Irish shores.

Andrew's Lane Theatre `25 G8`
9-17 St Andrew's Lane, Dublin 2
Phone 679 5720

Bewley's Cafe Theatre `25 G8`
2nd floor at Bewley's on Grafton Street
Phone 086 878 4001
Lunchtime drama - admission price includes soup and a sandwich.

Civic Theatre
Blessington Road, Dublin 24
Phone 462 7477

Draiocht
The Blanchardstown Centre, Dublin 15
Phone 885 2622

Gaiety Theatre `25 G8`
South King Street, Dublin 2
Phone 677 1717

Gate Theatre `17 G6`
1 Cavendish Row, Dublin 1
Phone 874 4045

The Helix `7 G3`
Collins Ave, Dublin 9
Phone 700 7000

The New Theatre `25 G7`
43 East Essex Street, Dublin 2
Phone 670 3361

Olympia Theatre `25 G7`
72 Dame Street, Dublin 2
Phone 679 3323

Pavilion Theatre `41 R13`
Marine Road, Dun Laoghaire
Phone 231 2929

Peacock Theatre `25 G7`
Lower Abbey Street, Dublin 1
Phone 878 7222

Project Arts Centre `25 G7`
39 East Essex St, Dublin 2
Phone 881 9614

Samuel Beckett Theatre `25 G7`
Trinity College, College Gn, Dublin 2
Phone 896 2461

Tivoli Theatre `24 F8`
135-138 Francis Street
Phone 454 4472

MUSIC

Music is very close to Irish hearts and it is almost impossible to visit Dublin without experiencing a musical encounter of one sort or another. From the buskers of Grafton Street and Temple Bar to the pubs and concert halls, there is always somebody close at hand, eager to play a tune or two.

Traditional Irish music remains very popular with locals and visitors alike, and a multitude of pubs have live sessions on a regular basis. Ireland also has a strange love affair with country & western music, but it is in the field of rock and popular music that the Irish have made their presence felt on the world stage in recent years with bands such as U2, The Cranberries, Westlife and The Corrs, and individuals such as Van Morrison, Bob Geldof, Ronan Keating, Sinéad O'Connor and Enya, to name but a few.

Dublin is a regular tour stop for these and a host of international recording artists. Most of the big acts play at The Point, but large concerts also take place occasionally at Dublin's three major outdoor sporting arenas, Lansdowne Road, Croke Park and the RDS. There are quite a few good mid-sized venues which include the Olympia Theatre, Vicar Street, Whelan's, the POD, the Button Factory and the

Ambassador. The HMV music stores on Grafton Street and Henry Street are good places to buy tickets in advance of the show, or try Ticketmaster who have outlets at St Stephen's Green Shopping Centre and the Jervis Centre. On a day to day basis, however, Dublin pubs and clubs provide the venues and cater to all musical persuasions, including rock, country, jazz and traditional. For more details, see pages 82-88.

For lovers of classical music, the main venue is the National Concert Hall which is home to the National Symphony Orchestra which plays most Friday evenings. The venue will remain open during a redevelopment programme which is due to be completed in 2013. Other performers, both amateurs and touring professionals, take to the stage in the main auditorium throughout the week. A wide variety of smaller concerts and lunchtime recitals takes place in the adjoining John Field Room which doubles up as the Concert Hall's bar area.

Construction of the National Convention Centre and Point Village

Other venues for classical music include the Hugh Lane Gallery and the National Gallery of Ireland. If you can't get hold of a free copy of *The Event Guide*, the Irish Times is a good place to track down performances. If you prefer the great outdoors, Dublin City Council sponsor free Music in the Parks on Sunday afternoons during the summer months. Details of forthcoming events are available on the noticeboard in St Stephen's Green.

Dublin, unfortunately, does not have an opera house but Opera Ireland perform two short seasons every spring and autumn at the Gaiety Theatre. Rather ironically, the operatic highlight of the year is the Wexford Festival Opera, which takes place during the last two weeks of October. If you prefer church music, choral concerts and organ recitals are a regular feature at both St Patrick's and Christ Church Cathedrals.

National Concert Hall   `31 H9`
Earlsfort Terrace, Dublin 2
Phone 417 0000

The Point   `26 J7`
North Wall Quay, Dublin 1
Phone 676 6144
Recent €80m redevelopment

The Button Factory   `25 G7`
Curved Street, Temple Bar, Dublin 2
Phone 670 9202

The POD/Tripod/Crawdaddy   `31 G8`
Old Harcourt Station
Harcourt Street, Dublin 2,
Phone 476 3374

CINEMA

With the help of tax incentives provided by the government, the Irish film industry has managed to establish a niche for itself, with many notable successes such as *The Commitments*, *Braveheart* and *Saving Private Ryan*. Cinema attendances have soared in recent years and the Irish now go to the 'flicks' as often as anybody else in Europe. The number of screens in and around the city has mushroomed with the opening of several new multiplexes.

Cinema HQ is the Irish Film Institute on Eustace Street (phone 679 3477) which opened in 1992 and is the main outlet for foreign language and art-house films, although the Screen on D'Olier Street also does its bit to break the Hollywood monopoly. The IFI is technically a members only club for over-18's, but the reality is that you simply pay €1 to be a member for a day, or €20 for annual membership. Its club status means that uncertified films are occasionally screened as the IFI does not have to submit all of its films to the censor.

Finally, a couple of tips regarding cost. As a general rule, if you want to save a few bob, go to the cinema in the afternoon and you will get in for around

two thirds of what it costs in the evening. If you are totally skint, free films are screened by the IFI outdoors on Saturday nights during July and August in Meeting House Square in Temple Bar. Each film is chosen by an invited celeb who addresses the audience before the film begins. Tickets can be obtained from the Temple Bar Cultural Information Centre on East Essex Street.

COMEDY

Ireland has produced a rich crop of stand-up comedians in recent years including Ardal O'Hanlon, Sean Hughes, Dylan Moran, Tommy Tiernan, Ed Byrne, Graham Norton, and Dara O'Briain. It has to be said that most of these acts were actually blooded on the London comedy circuit, but Dublin does have one or two good venues of its own which are helping to keep the production line rolling.

The most established is the International Bar on Wicklow Street (phone 677 9250) which hosts stand-up most nights of the week upstairs in the Comedy Cellar. Other venues include the Ha'penny Bridge Inn on Wellington Quay (phone 677 0616) which stages a twice weekly show on Tuesday and Thursday nights. Larger scale venues which host some of the bigger acts when they are visiting town include the Olympia Theatre, the Ambassador and Vicar Street.

ANGLING

There is fresh water fishing on certain stretches of the River Liffey for salmon, trout, pike and perch. The River Tolka is also popular with trout fishermen and there is some coarse fishing on Dublin's two canals. Fishing permits are available from tackle shops. Howth and Dun Laoghaire are the main centres for sea fishing.

BOWLING

There are several ten pin bowling alleys in and around Dublin, many of which are open 24 hours a day. Stillorgan has the oldest bowling alley in Ireland and it hosts all the major competitions including the Irish Open. Prices depend on the day and time, but the cheapest period is usually before 6pm on weekdays.

Leisureplex
Old Bray Rd, Stillorgan, Co Dublin
Phone 288 1656

Leisureplex `9 M2`
Malahide Road, Coolock,
Dublin 17
Phone 848 5722

Outdoor bowling greens are in short supply in Dublin, but there's one in Moran Park in Dun Laoghaire and another, which is closer to the centre of town, in Herbert Park in Ballsbridge.

CYCLING

There is a strong cycling tradition in Ireland which was recognised in 1998 when the Tour de France held its first stage in Dublin to honour the international success of Sean Kelly and Stephen Roche. The biggest domestic event is the Tour of Ireland which normally takes place at the end of August, starting in Dublin.

There are no indoor cycling arenas in the city but there is an outdoor track in Eamon Ceannt Park on Sundrive Road in Crumlin which is open to the public (www.cyclingireland.ie). If you simply want to hire a bike and do a bit of exploring, there are several bike hire shops in and around the city. See page 66.

GAELIC GAMES

Gaelic football and hurling are Ireland's two national sports, and both have their headquarters at Croke Park which is Ireland's finest sports stadium (phone 836 3222). Both games retain their amateur status and are governed by the Gaelic Athletic Association (GAA) which was founded in 1884 to promote indigenous games. In doing so, its aim was to forge a distinctive Irish identity during a period of British rule in Ireland.

Gaelic football is a fast and physical game, often likened to Australian Rules football which itself evolved from Irish roots, although the Irish play with a round ball. Ireland's 32 counties compete for a place in the All Ireland Final which takes place at Croke in September in front of 80,000 spectators. Tickets for the final are very hard to come by but a trip to one of the earlier rounds at Croke Park will provide a flavour of the event. Parnell Park in Donnycarney is a good place to catch big club games which generally take place on Saturday evenings during the summer months and Sunday afternoons during the winter (phone 831 0066). The All Ireland club finals take place at Croke Park on 17th March, St Patrick's Day.

Hurling is played with a stick and a ball, or *sliothar* (pronounced slitter), and is a game of great skill and co-ordination, despite taking on the appearance of open warfare at times. The All Ireland hurling final is also staged in September at Croke Park.

GOLF

Unlike the situation in many other countries, golf is not an elitist game in Ireland. Many of the world's finest courses are close to hand but there are many alternatives to suit players of all abilities. Green fees at the top end of the market can be very expensive, but elsewhere they are rarely prohibitive. Royal Dublin and Portmarnock are two Dublin courses which have long enjoyed international renown, and they have more recently been joined by the K Club in County Kildare (the stage for Europe's victory in the 2006 Ryder Cup), Druids Glen and the European Club, both of which are in County Wicklow. Other fine courses in and around the city include Grange Castle, Hermitage, the Island, Malahide, Milltown and Woodbrook. These clubs are all private, but visitors are welcome, especially during the week. Municipal courses offer a cheaper alternative, and there are a num-

ber of par-3 and pitch and putt courses dotted around the city. If you want to see how the game really should be played, take a trip to the Irish Open which is one of the leading tournaments on the European Tour, attracting many of the world's top players. The venue changes, as does the timing, but the event is currently staged in late May.

GREYHOUND RACING

Greyhound racing is very popular in Ireland and meetings are staged all year round at Dublin's two main tracks.

Shelbourne Park Stadium `26 J8`
South Lotts Road, Dublin 4
Phone 668 3502
Stages meetings every Wednesday, Thursday and Saturday night.

Harold's Cross Stadium `30 F10`
Harold's Cross Road, Dublin 6W
Phone 497 1081
Stages meetings every Monday, Tuesday and Friday nights.

HORSE RACING & RIDING

Ireland is famous around the globe for breeding and training some of the world's greatest thoroughbreds (and it produces a few good horses into the bargain). Many Dubliners enjoy a flutter on the horses and the most convenient place for them to be parted from their cash is Leopardstown racecourse which is only 6 miles from the city centre in the suburb of Foxrock (phone 289 3607). The annual highlights are the Hennessy Gold Cup which takes place in February and, a must for all cabin fever sufferers, the Leopardstown Festival meeting which starts on Boxing Day and runs for 4 days.

The Irish Grand National is run on Easter Monday at Fairyhouse which is about 15 miles north of the city (phone 825 6167). The headquarters of Irish flat racing is 30 miles south west of Dublin at the Curragh which hosts all five Classics, including the Irish Derby which is a major social occasion. Other courses within an hour's drive of Dublin include Naas and Punchestown which are both in County Kildare. All national newspapers carry details of the day's race meetings and special buses run from Busaras on race days.

Away from the track, the RDS

(Royal Dublin Society) hosts the Dublin Horse Show each year in August. This is a major international show jumping event which attracts hundreds of competitors from around the world and thousands of spectators. If you prefer riding them to betting on them, there are many riding centres in and around Dublin, including Brennanstown Riding School near Bray which offers cross-country rides in the scenic Wicklow Hills. For more information, phone 286 3778.

descend on Dublin for the weekend help to turn these matches into a great social occasion.

SNOOKER

There are quite a few snooker halls in and around the city, the most famous of which is Jason's of Ranelagh (phone 497 5983), home to Ken Doherty, world champion in 1997, and finalist in 2003. A full list of clubs and halls can be found in the Golden Pages.

KARTING

Budding Formula 1 drivers of all ages can hone their skills on indoor circuits. Advanced booking is recommended as karting has become a very popular corporate junket, and the circuits are sometimes entirely booked up for the event.

Kart City
Old Airport Road, Santry, Dublin 9
Phone 842 6322
400 metre track and a 700 metre outdoor track where the karts can reach speeds of up to 80kph. Other facilities at the site include **Urban Paintball** and **Rampcity**, the biggest indoor skatepark in the country. Open Mon-Fri 2pm-10pm, Sat & Sun 12noon-10pm

Kylemore Karting Centre
Kylemore Industrial Estate
Killeen Road, Dublin 10   `28 A10`
Phone 626 1444
Two 360 metre indoor tracks. Open Mon-Sun 11am until late.

RUGBY

Lansdowne Road in Ballsbridge is the headquarters of the Irish Rugby Football Union (phone 647 3800). The stadium is currently being transformed from a rather archaic venue into a 50,000 all-seater, state of the art facility due for completion in 2010. Not without controversy, Croke Park has provided rugby with a temporary home in the meantime. The highlight of the year is the Six Nations Championship which takes place during February and March when Ireland take on England, Scotland, Wales, France and Italy. Irish fortunes were on the up until a disastrous World Cup in 2007 but, even when there is a conspicuous lack of Irish success on the field, tickets are very difficult to acquire. The thousands of foreign invaders who

SOCCER

For many years Irish soccer lived in the shadow of Gaelic games until big Jack (Charlton) came from England, of all places, to manage the national side. Ten years of unprecedented success in the European Championships and the World Cup gripped the nation. Jack returned to his fishing rod and the team was guided by Mick McCarthy to the 2002 World Cup finals, during which time the Irish public was once again seized by the drama, both on and off the pitch. The drama later made it onto stage with a smash-hit musical, *I Keano*, based on a bust-up between Mick and his eloquent captain, Roy Keane.

Brian Kerr and Steve Staunton came and went without success, and Geovanni Trapatoni currently has a tenuous grasp of the reins. But there is no sign of interest waning. International matches are being played at Croke Park until the redevelopment of Lansdowne Road is completed in 2010 The headquarters of the Football Association of Ireland are at 80 Merrion Square (ph 676 6864).

The top three Dublin teams are Bohemians who play at Dalymount Park in Phibsborough, St Patrick's Athletic who play at Richmond Park in Inchicore, and Shamrock Rovers who play at Tolka Park in Drumcondra. All three play in the Premier Division of the Eircom League of Ireland, usually on Sundays, but support for local league sides is dwarfed by the passionate interest which Dubliners take in the English Premiership.

SWIMMING & WATER SPORTS

If you aren't afraid of cold water, there are good beaches just outside the city at Portmarnock and Balbriggan to the north, and Killiney to the south. Alternatively, the Forty Foot Pool offers

Gaelic football at Croke Park

a rare opportunity to immerse yourself in both the Irish Sea and Irish literature. Follow in the footsteps of Buck Mulligan who went there for a bracing dip in James Joyce's novel, *Ulysses*. The pool, which is named after the 40th Regiment of Foot who used to be stationed nearby, is overlooked by the Joyce Tower and is easily reached by taking the DART to Sandycove. If you aren't feeling quite so hardy, there's a decent indoor pool at Markievicz Leisure Centre on Townsend Street (phone 672 9121). A full list of indoor swimming pools can be found in the Golden Pages.

Sailing is a popular activity, especially around Howth and Dun Laoghaire, but sailing clubs are usually restricted to members only. The Irish National Sailing School, however, offers courses for all levels throughout the year. The school is situated by Dun Laoghaire's West Pier (phone 284 4195). Wind surfing is another popular activity in this area of town and equipment and tuition are available from Wind & Wave Watersports in Monkstown (phone 284 4177).

TENNIS

Since most tennis clubs are privately run for the benefit of members and their guests, the most realistic option is a game in one of the city's parks. There are public courts at Bushy Park on Rathdown Avenue in Terenure (phone 490 0320), Herbert Park in Ballsbridge (phone 668 4364) and in St Anne's Park in Raheny (833 8898).

Dublin shops generally open Monday to Saturday from 9am to 6pm, with late shopping in the city centre on Thursday until 8pm. Many city centre department stores and book shops open on Sunday, usually from 10am until 7pm. Visitors from outside the European Community can claim a rebate on the purchase price of items carrying Value Added Tax. Inquire at the time of purchase for more details.

Fashion

Despite centuries of acrimonious history, the latest English invasion has been bloodless. However, while Dublin city centre may incorporate the chain stores of any English high street, they do not dominate street style.

There are several predominantly pedestrianised shopping areas, central of which is **Grafton Street**, where the electronic whir of ATMs and debit card validation machines is subdued by buskers, poets, jugglers, flowers sellers and the odd north Dublin urchin singing the Fields of Athenry.

Brown Thomas department store is a vibrant and surprisingly unsnobbish slice of Dublin life. Apart from the luxurious, international designer floor, you are as likely to find tourists and school girls in their frumpy convent school uniforms as fashionistas trying out the cosmetics, shoes and accessible designers such as **Joseph, Whistles, Day** and **Antik Batik**. Irish designers **Orla Kiely** and **Quinn & Donnelly** get their share of the coveted market.

Further up Grafton Street, the abbreviated **BT2** features the more casual designer end of the spectrum, while next door is the company's cheaper in-house label, **A Wear**. Linking Grafton Street with Dawson Street is **Hibernian Way**, flanked by the men's design stalwart **Alias Tom**, encompassing a number of boutiques including sophisticated American store **Meg**, boho, laid back lifestyle shop **Potrero Hill**, and designer shoe shop **Cocobelle**. Link back to Grafton Street via Anne Street South with monied country casual **Hackett**.

Further on, the talented **Pia Bang** has survived where many have been taken over by the chain store multiples. The chic **Richard Allen** is also a long term survivor, with foot fetishists catered for by the elegant **Carl Scarpa**, zany **Zerep** and tub thumping **Korky.** At the top, opposite St Stephen's Green, **Reiss** and **Coast** are joined by the fashion magazines' favourite, **Top Shop**. That part of the green is dominated by the St Stephen's Green Shopping Centre, thronged by mall rats and their harassed parents, and housing a large and convenient branch of **Dunnes Stores.** Apart from the rummager's paradise of **TK Maxx**, most of the shops are aimed at the young, street look.

At the other end of Grafton Street, **Wicklow Street** is burgeoning into more than just a thoroughfare to somewhere else. **Chesneau** supplies elegant, simple, investment handbags. **Cinders** displays an array of shoes with surprisingly modest price tags. **Sabotage** represents the young, casually fashion conscious, while **Magee** is successfully reviving its tweedy image. **Louis Copeland**, opposite, is tailor to politicians and celebrities, with branches in Pembroke Street Lower, Capel Street and CHQ.

Adjacent **Suffolk Street** is home to **Avoca**, a surreal, Ballykissangel, girlie, emporium of clothing, accessories, gifts, food and a superb café. The antithesis of the soulless, industrial neighbouring **Diesel** store. Round the corner, into **Dame Lane**, the staff in **Lara**, get the vote for making their customers feel welcome.

Across into **Nassau Street**, don't be put off by the Oirish shops or the preppy sub Gap **Farrell and Brown**, and stride firmly towards the **Kilkenny Design Centre**. Gone are the lumpy Aran sweaters to be replaced by slick marketing of 21st century Ireland, such as **Orla Kiely, Aileen Bodkin**, the wedding list must haves of **John Rocha Waterford Crystal** and the original Kilkenny craft designers, topped by a great café.

Back off Grafton Street, Harry Street houses the decadently overstuffed **Rococco**, the **Berry Brothers** and **Rudd** wine shop, and the beautifully co-ordinated clothes from **Noa Noa**. This leads into the **Westbury Mall**, primarily known for jewellery, but also with two branches of the sexy, colourful **Chica**

and bizarrely named **Shag.**

Now the shopper is facing the beautiful old **Powerscourt Townhouse**, filled with opportunities for retail therapy via **French Connection**, the glamourously quirky **All Saints**, and, on the top floor, the **Design Centre**. No longer solely the showcase for Irish designers, the centre plus the adjacent seductive **Coco**, are *the* places to go if you have to look particularly fabulous. An evolving space is **Loft** with stalls of new Irish designer and vintage pieces. Stall owners sit around chatting, some while knitting and making jewellery. It is the noughties version of the Arran Island piece worker. All the quirkiness of London's Dover Street Market with none of the prices.

Similarly the surrounding **Castle Market** is home to the lavish **Costume**, opposite the stylish **Number 6**, selling the likes of Helen Mc Alinden and nearby **Drury Street** for occasionwear in **Caru**, the decadent, shoe boudoir, **Cherche Midi**, the fabulous **Smock** and Greenwich village ambience of **Alila**. Less money may be needed to shop in the **George's Street Market Arcade**, but there is no shortage of food stalls, including a redolent gourmet olive stall, book and record stalls plus several inexpensive but highly individual clothes stores.

Head towards the river and you enter **Temple Bar**. While at night a seething mass of drunken, underclothed, stag and hen parties, during the day it is a pleasant stroll taking in **Urban Outfitters**, comprising floors of cool kitsch and ethnic **Takara**. There is still a student air around the cobbled streets, with shops selling clothes that previously would have been described as second hand, but are now " vintage."

At the far end of Temple Bar, Saturday sees a fledgling fashion market in **Cow's Lane**, incongruously surrounded by new apartment blocks and contemporary furniture shops. **Claire Garvey** designs Irish fantasy dresses influenced by Jim Fitzgerald.

On the other side of the River Liffey, via the Millennium Bridge, the ludicrously titled **Quartiere Bloom** sprinkles a little of *la dolce vita* at **La Bottega** Italian delicatessen, curiously interspersed with **Sabotage** clothing and **Buddha Bag** bean bags, and leads you to the English **Jervis** shopping centre which then faces **Henry Street**. This area has been upgraded by major investment into the **Arnotts** department store and the previously dowdy **Ilac Centre** with **Zara** and **H & M**. There are fewer tourists but with Grafton Street rents now stratospheric this is where the Dubliner shops. Back onto **O'Connell Street**, dominated by the famous spire,

Saturday's Temple Bar food market

there is less of interest to the shopper other than the cheap but currently fashionable **Penneys**. Further along the river, the new financial district houses the **CHQ** building. The hike is rewarded by **Ciaran Sweeney**'s sumptuous textiles, the dressy **Kohl, The Pink Room** or **Fitzpatricks** for shoes and SATC dressing up box, **Fran and Jane**

Irish milliner, Philip Treacey, may have the royal seal of approval but internationally known Irish designers are rare. Northerner, Paul Costelloe, made a brief bid for fame with further royal patronage. John Rocha can do no wrong, but we sort of borrowed him from Hong Kong. The current holder of the international title is **Louise Kennedy**, who has dressed the last two Irish presidents, both stylish women, and Cherie Blair who, bless her, needs all the help she can get. A Georgian townhouse at 56 Merrion Square contains her trademark, precision tailored daywear, sumptuous evening clothes and signature Tipperary crystal.

The suburbs have always had their classy boutiques such as **Rococco** in Glasthule, **Anthologie** in Clontarf, **Venezuela** in Skerries, **Anastasia** and **Kelli** in Ranelagh or **Khan** in Blackrock, but Dundrum poached the real cash cow, the **Dundrum Town Centre,** an enormous, mother of all shopping centres. Built around **Tesco, M & S** and a disappointingly provincial, but recently revamped **House of Fraser**, the centre covers every high street multiple you have ever heard of. Individual or Irish based based shops are few and far between. If you hate shopping centres, be warned, this could be pure hell, but if you love them, this is the ultimate, with promises of greater things to come in a more upmarket designer section. Currently the *piece de resistance* is quite a small branch of **Harvey Nichols** with comparatively spacious pop art furnished café and stylish restaurant with dance floor. Whether or not Irish man is quite ready for that, the siting of the latest Harvey Nichols in Dublin does reflect the affluence and style of the Irish in the international arena. Multicultural, and particularly European influence has been adopted and adapted in cuisine, wine, design, and now clothing, lessening the threatened globalisation blandness of many cities.

Books

Dublin lives up to its literary reputation with a rich selection of book shops, many of which open seven days a week and close later than most other shops. Dawson Street is home to two of the heavyweights, **Waterstones** and **Hodges & Figgis**. Around the corner in Nassau

A quiet Sunday on Grafton Street - Dublin's College of Retail Therapy

Street, **Reads** have a large outlet and plenty of discounts. **Dubray Books** on Grafton Street, **Hughes & Hughes** in St Stephen's Green Shopping Centre, and **Books Upstairs** on College Green are all well stocked and centrally located. **Easons**, with stores on O'Connell Street and throughout Ireland, sell an excellent range of books, newspapers, magazines, stationery, art materials and a variety of other goods.

Irish Crafts & Textiles

Ireland has a long tradition for producing excellent craftware with producers such as Waterford Crystal and Belleek Pottery firmly established in markets all around the world. As mentioned earlier, the **Kilkenny Shop** on Nassau Street has modernised both its stock and its approach in recent years and now ranks as Dublin's leading outlet for Irish craftware. One side of the shop specialises in clothes - mainly woollens, tweeds and linen while the rest of the shop is dedcated to Irish glass, pottery, ceramics and metalwork. The **Blarney Woollen Mills**, also on Nassau Street, follows a similar layout while other outlets noted for their fine selection of Irish woollens are the **Sweatershop** on Wicklow Street and **Dublin Woollen Mills** on Lower Ormond Quay.

The **Crafts Council Gallery** in the Powerscourt Townhouse displays and sells a wide range of crafts by Irish and international designers, and the **Tower Design Centre** on Pearse Street houses a number of studios for craft workers, producing jewellery, ceramics, fabrics, and other hand-crafted items.

Behind Christchurch, in the area

known as the **Liberties**, there are generally thin pickings for the intrepid shopper, apart from antiques on **Francis Street**, broken by a pick-you-up- coffee, home made quiche or delicious cake in the **Gallic Kitchen**.

Music

Dublin may be the city of a thousand bands but musical retailing is dominated by British superstores. **Virgin** have one of their Megastores on Aston Quay, and **HMV** have branches on Grafton St and Henry St. **Golden Discs**, an Irish chain, have several branches around the city. Temple Bar offers some welcome relief from the big players with a growing number of independent music retailers, many catering to specific tastes. **Claddagh Records** on Cecilia St, for example, is famous for its collection of Irish traditional and folk music. **Celtic Note** on Nassau St also lures passing trade.

Markets

The famous **Moore Street Market**, operates from Monday to Saturday and specialises in fruit, vegetables and flowers. Across the river, the **Temple Bar Food Market** is held every Saturday in Meeting House Square and appeals more to the stuffed olive brigade with an impressive array of speciality foods on offer. If you are seeking shelter, there is plenty of variety on offer in the covered market in **George's Arcade**, between South Great George's St and Drury St. Further out of town, **Blackrock** hosts a large market every Saturday and Sunday which attracts a good crowd to its diverse range of stalls.

Dublin offers many forms of entertainment, but the heart and soul of the city's social life is undoubtedly the pub, with nearly a thousand to choose from.

Many have changed very little over the past 100 years, and many more have tried to recapture the past, but an increasing number are looking to the future with a strong European influence taking hold. Dublin is arguably the best city in the world for pubs but the primary reason for their allure is the wide cross-section of people who work and drink there.

The selection of pubs, clubs and bars below tries to point you in the direction of some of Dublin's finest watering holes but, if you feel strongly that any have been wrongly included or unfairly omitted, feel free to let us know. Most of the pubs listed serve food, and many stage live music. To find out who is playing when and where, pick up a copy of *The Event Guide*, a free paper published every two weeks and available at many pubs and bars across town. If you are on-line, try www.entertainment.ie for reviews and listings.

The list below is NOT broken into categories as so many of Dublin's bars and clubs fall into more than one bracket. Many bars become a nightclub so that you can carry on drinking until late.

Opening hours have been omitted as they are often subject to extensions which can vary according to what's on. Pubs normally open from 10.30am to 11.30pm from Monday to Thursday, 10.30am-12.30am Friday & Saturday, and from 12noon to 11pm on Sunday. Many pubs have a late licence at weekends and serve until 1.30am. Nightclubs normally serve until 2.30am, but bear in mind that it might be cheaper and as much fun to stay on in the pub.

By law, drink prices should be displayed outside licensed premises but, if you miss them on the way in, a good rule of thumb is to expect extortionate prices (the theory is that the shock will drive you to drink). To add further insult, prices are sometimes hiked later in the evening, and a premium is often added for cheapskates who have the temerity to drink half pints.

When it comes to beer, Guinness reigns supreme in Dublin. Brewed at St James's Gate, many Dubliners spend much of their life in search of the perfect pint. Where the Japanese have their tea ceremony, Irish barmen perform their own ritual when pouring a pint of the black stuff but, like all good things in life, it is usually worth waiting for. Competition is at hand in the form of Beamish and Murphys, both of which are brewed in Cork, and there are plenty of foreign lagers to choose from. If you pre-

fer a pint of ale, Smithwicks and Kilkenny dominate the market, both brewed by none other than Guinness!

The Temple Bar area has the highest concentration of pubs in the city and it tends to act as a honey pot for tourists, many of whom seem to be enjoying their last hours of freedom, although stag and hen parties have recently been banned by many Temple Bar establishments. If things are getting a bit tired and emotional, you need only walk a couple of hundred yards to escape the mayhem. As city centre pubs are busy most nights of the week, a hotel bar is often a good bet if you are looking for a quiet drink. Bear in mind, though, that there is no such thing as a quiet drink in Dublin come Friday and Saturday night.

Don't be put off by the sight of people crowding around the entrance to a bar - it may look like a queue or a doormen's convention, but it is more likely to be a group of 'snoutcasts', forced outdoors by the introduction of a nationwide smoking ban in pubs and restaurants back in 2004. The ban has been implemented with little fuss, and non-smokers have been known to infiltrate the ranks outside to take advantage of the flirting opportunities. Most publicans complain that the ban has damaged their business, but some are enjoying an increase in turnover due to the fact that many people are turning their backs on expensive restaurants and eating in pubs that would have been too smoky before the ban.

Finally, if you like to keep on the move but aren't sure where you are going, there are some well organised pub crawls. The **Dublin Literary Pub Crawl** is conducted by professional actors who will bring you to a selection of Dublin's best known literary pubs, and enlighten you with performances from the works

Phil Lynott at the Bruxelles

of Joyce, Beckett and Behan, among many others. The evening kicks off at the Duke on Duke Street at 7.30pm every night from April to November, at 7.30pm Thursday to Sunday during the rest of the year, and at 12noon on Sundays all year round. Tickets cost €12. If you prefer music to literature, the **Musical Pub Crawl** starts at 7.30 pm every night from April to October upstairs at Oliver St John Gogarty's on Fleet Street. The winter schedule is limited to Thursday, Friday and Saturday nights from November through to March. Tickets cost €12.

If you would rather organise your own pub crawl, then feel free to work your way through the list below!

4 Dame Lane   `25 G7`
4 Dame Lane, Dublin 2
Phone 679 0291
Impressive bar, similar in feel to Dakota, but with the added bonus of additional lounging space upstairs. DJ's help to make it an in place at weekends. Quieter during the week due to its tucked away location. Free wi-fi.

Anseo   `25 G8`
8 Camden Street Lower, Dublin 2
Phone 475 1321
One of several old style boozers around town that have been turned around by the introduction of DJ's and a music policy that pulls in an assortment of trendy young things. Low budget but a cool place.

The Bailey   `25 G8`
2-3 Duke Street, Dublin 2
Phone 670 4939
Located just off Grafton Street, the Bailey has an unrivalled literary tradition which stretches back to the mid-19th century. Former patrons include Joyce, Yeats, and Behan, as well as Michael Collins, the evasive IRA General, who drank upstairs while on the run from the British military who were drinking downstairs! The pub no longer trades off these associations, however. Following the redevelopment of Marks & Spencers next door, the refurbished Bailey has dispensed with the literary memorabilia and opted instead for a chic 21st century interior. The clientele are smart and cosmopolitan, and include plenty of Dubliners who like to recover here after a hard day at the office.

The Bank   `25 G7`
22 College Green
Phone 677 0677
The only way to afford an interior like this is to make sure that the bank has already paid for most of it. Retains many of the original features of this former

banking hall; mosaic floor, ornate plasterwork, vaulted ceilings and stained glass skylights. Large oval bar dominates the centre of the room, with additional seating on a mezzanine level. Popular stop for shop and office workers after a hard day at the coal face.

The Bleeding Horse `31 G9`
24 Upper Camden Street, Dublin 2
Phone 475 2705
There has been a pub here since the days of Oliver Cromwell but the current building dates back only to the last century. Popular with nearby office workers by day, and a good crowd usually takes advantage of the late night bar every Friday and Saturday.

The Bloody Stream `13 V2`
14 West Pier, Howth
Phone 839 5076
Step off the DART in the attractive fishing village of Howth, step straight into the Bloody Stream, take a seat, indoors or out, order a pint, a bowl of chowder and a seafood platter from the friendly staff, and all will be well with the world. Guaranteed.

Bowes `25 G7`
31 Fleet Street, Dublin 2
Phone 671 4038
Fleet Street is fortunate to have two pubs that are true gems. Bowes, like the nearby Palace, is small but beautifully formed with lots of carved wood, plenty of old-school character, and a few old-school characters for that matter.

The Brazen Head `24 F7`
20 Lower Bridge St, Dublin 8
Phone 679 5186
Located at the end of a cobbled courtyard across the river from the Four Courts, the Brazen Head enjoys the accolade of being Dublin's oldest pub, although its exact age is a matter of some dispute. The pub sign claims the year 1198 but this actually relates to an earlier tavern which used to occupy the same site. A labyrinth of low-ceilinged, smoke-stained rooms makes up the current building which is thought to date back to the early eighteenth century. This is a no frills type of bar, but nightly sessions of traditional music help to pull the punters in after dark.

The Bruxelles `25 G8`
7 Harry Street, Dublin 2
Phone 677 5362
An attractive Victorian interior, slightly cramped at times, and a few tables outside if you are hoping to catch a few rays or a nicotine hit. A prime location, just off Grafton Street, helps to keep things busy both day and night. Live music.

Terrace drinkers at the Church on Mary Street

The Button Factory `25 G7`
Curved Street, Temple Bar, Dublin 2
Phone 670 9202
Formerly the Temple Bar Music Centre, a refurb and relaunch have enhanced the facilities which should ensure that it remains in the forefront of Dublin's live music venues.

Café en Seine `25 H8`
39-40 Dawson Street, Dublin 2
Phone 677 4567
When it first opened in 1993, Café en Seine quickly established itself as many people's favourite Dublin watering hole. Following its expansion into the building next door, it doubled in size but lost none of its appeal. The slightly over the top, art deco interior evokes a *fin de siecle* feel which earned it the moniker 'Cafe Insane', but it continues to attract well heeled punters like bees to honey.

Cellar Bar `25 H8`
Upper Merrion St, Dublin 2
Phone 603 0600
Stone and brick arched vault underneath the upmarket Merrion Hotel (bar has its own separate entrance). Good place to take a discerning mistress - she will be impressed with your largesse, and your extra curricular activities are unlikely to come to light in these intimate and discrete surroundings.

The Church `25 G7`
Mary Street, Dublin 1
Phone 828 0102
Sympathetic, yet spectacular, conversion of an 18th century Church of Ireland church which retains many original features, including acres of stained glass and an organ played by Handel prior to

the first performance of his *Messiah* in 1742. Beautiful main bar at ground floor level, large outdoor terrace which really comes into its own when the sun is shining, restaurant at mezzanine level, and late night club in the basement.

The Cobblestone `24 F7`
77 North King St, Smithfield, Dublin 7
Phone 872 1799
One of the few period buildings left standing (just about) in this area of urban regeneration. Old fashioned Dublin boozer offering a daily diet of live music, mainly traditional.

Dakota `25 G8`
8-9 South William St, Dublin 2
Phone 672 7690
Cavernous bar, with acres of exposed brickwork, polished wooden floors and leather upholstered alcoves, but manages to be warm, hip and happening. Great vibe, attractive crowd of twenty and thirtysomethings, and an outdoor terrace if you're gasping for a ciggie. Late bar Thursday, Friday & Saturday.

Davy Byrne's `25 G8`
21 Duke Street, Dublin 2

---

5 For Tradition

The Stag's Head
Mulligan's
The Palace Bar
Doheny & Nesbitt
The Long Hall

Spread your wings at the Market Bar on Fade Street

Phone 677 5217
James Joyce immortalised a few Dublin pubs in his time and, yes, this is another one. Described in *Ulysses*, as 'a moral pub', it has has undergone considerable change since it opened in 1873 - physically, rather than morally, of course. There are now three bars, all refurbished to reflect more modern times, but still retaining a few connections with the past. Davy Byrne, who ran the bar for more than 50 years, appears in one of the murals which were painted by Brendan Behan's father-in-law, no less! The pub's central location, just off Grafton Street, and its reputation for good pub food helps to keep it popular with businessmen, shoppers and tourists alike. Look out for Joyce enthusiasts, dressed in

Ron Black's on Dawson Street

Edwardian attire, as they celebrate Bloomsday on 14th June every year.

Dice Bar   24 F7
79 Queen Street, Dublin 7
Phone 872 8622
Part-owned by Huey from the Fun Lovin' Criminals, there's a strong hint of New York in this dimly lit bar, partly because of its slightly gritty location in the heart of Smithfield. DJ's and a rather soulful playlist attract a laid back crowd.

Dicey's Garden   25 G8
21-25 Harcourt Street, Dublin 2
Phone 478 4066
Hidden behind the imposing Georgian façade of the Russell Court Hotel is probably the best appointed outdoor drinking space in Dublin. Bar, barbeque, plasma screens and a forest of gas heaters to ward off the goose bumps.

Doheny & Nesbitt   25 H8
5 Lower Baggot St, Dublin 2
Phone 676 2945
Much unimproved! - Nesbitt's is very much the genuine article when it comes to an early Victorian pub, right down to the bare floor boards, smoke stained ceilings, and a bar complete with wooden partitions. Situated around the corner from the Irish Parliament, this is a favourite watering hole for lawyers, politicians and the press pack, but it manages to overcome these drawbacks with considerable ease.

The Duke   25 G8
9 Duke Street, Dublin 2
Phone 679 9553
Characterful pub, just off Grafton Street, and starting point for the Literary Pub

Crawl (see page 82).

The Dylan   32 J9
Eastmoreland Place, Dublin 4
Phone 660 3000
Dublin's trendiest boutique hotel and a popular spot to practise your posing while enjoying a cocktail or two in the small but sumptuous hotel bar.

Fagan's   17 H5
146 Drumcondra Road, Dublin 9
Phone 836 9491
Northside stalwart, most famous for being ex Taoiseach, Bertie Ahern's favourite watering hole. No doubt, Bill Clinton is forever propping up the bar at his own local.

Fallon & Byrne Wine Bar   25 G8
11-17 Exchequer Street, dublin 2
Phone 472 1010
Wine cellar where the wine list is stacked around you and complemented by tasty, and relatively inexpensive, plates of cheese and charcuterie. Very rare that four Dublin lads decide to share a bottle of wine - so, the hubbub is generated mainly by couples and girls out for a chinwag.

The Ferryman   26 J7
Sir John Rogerson's Quay, Dublin 2
Phone 671 7053
Strolling along the north side of the Liffey? Looking for adventure? Invest €2, and take the little ferry across to this traditional, but upwardly mobile, docklands bar on the south side of the river. The construction of Santiago Calatrava's Samuel Beckett Bridge should be good news for the bar, maybe not so good for the ferry man.

Fitzsimons   25 G7
East Essex Street, Temple Bar
Phone 677 9315
As they put it themselves, 'five floors of fun, food, frolics and sport'. A Temple Bar stalwart catering mainly to tourists with a daily diet of live music, DJ's, sport on a large screen, and dancing until 3am (2am on Sundays). Even the open-air roof terrace has a full bar.

Floridita   25 H7
Irish Life Mall, Abbey St, Dublin 1
Phone 878 1032
Havana meets Dublin with an upmarket mix of cocktail bar, restaurant and bands flown in from Cuba.

Front Lounge   25 G7
33-34 Parliament Street, Dublin 2
Phone 670 4112
Whether it's Front Lounge or Back Lounge depends on which entrance you prefer. This is a good place to escape the

Temple Bar throng, sink into one of the comfy sofas or armchairs, and cast an appreciative eye over the art, sculpture, and your fellow poseurs. Not exclusively gay, but certainly a gay-friendly bar.

The Gaiety Theatre   `25 G8`
South King St, Dublin 2
Phone 677 1717
Several Dublin theatres are turned over to late night clubbers on Friday and Saturday nights. The Gaiety makes use of the theatre bars to provide three floors of entertainment with different DJ's and live bands on each floor, while cult films are screened in the main auditorium. Doors open at 11.15 pm. The music is mainly salsa, soul, funk reggae & jazz. Bars stay open until 4am. Ground floor Plaza Cafe Bar is open during the day.

The Globe & Rí-Rá   `25 G8`
11 South Great George's Street, Dublin 2
Phone 671 1220
One of the first in a long succession of Dublin café bars, it doesn't open shop until mid afternoon these days, but it continues to draw a cool crowd. Late bar every night and free entrance to Rí-Rá (pronounced Ree-Raw) before 11.30pm, a nightclub where the door policy may be less exclusive than some, but the packed dance floors help to keep the temperature hot. Entrance to Rí-Rá is on Dame Court.

The George   `25 G8`
21 South Great George's St, Dublin 2
Phone 478 2983
Dublin's biggest, and best known gay venue. Bar and nightclub with a hectic schedule of music and entertainment.

Grogan's Castle Lounge   `25 G8`
15 South William Street, Dublin 2
Phone 677 9320
If Lidl was a bar, it might look like this. Definitely no frills, although that is perhaps unfair to the quirky art collection on the walls. Clientele are a mix of tourists and own brand local characters who look like they've been unavoidably detained on their way to an AA meeting. Great toasties, gem of a place.

Hairy Lemon   `25 G8`
42 Stephen Street Lower, Dublin 2
Phone 671 8949
Interior design by Steptoe & Son. Loads of interesting paraphernalia, and nooks and crannies galore. Forever busy.

Harbourmaster Bar   `25 H7`
IFSC, Dublin 1
Phone 670 1688
If you like the contrast of old and new, you will like this place which is set in the old Dock Offices building, bang in the middle of Dublin's financial district, with acres of steel and glass peering down from above. The dimly lit interior, which has been sensitively converted to its present use, is populated by quite a few of the suits who work nearby, but the atmosphere is laid back and unpretentious. Decent bar food is available or you can dine in the restaurant area which overlooks the dock basin outside.

Hartigans   `25 H8`
Lower Leeson Street, Dublin 2
Situated just off St Stephen's Green, an area where you would have to talk in telephone numbers to acquire a small piece of real estate, and yet Hartigan's is one of those traditional watering holes which doesn't seem to have splashed the cash anytime in the past 100 years. Long may it remain so.

Hole in the Wall   `23 D7`
Blackhorse Avenue, Dublin 7
Phone 838 9491
Originally a coach house dating back to 1610, this is as close as you'll get to finding a pub within the 1700 acres of Dublin's Phoenix Park. Increasingly focused on food, judging by the recent opening of a wine shop within the pub.

The Horseshoe Bar   `25 H8`
Shelbourne Hotel, St Stephen's Green
The city's grandest hotel has survived her facelift, and this windowless jewel has been recolonised by many of Dublin's power brokers, especially after work on a Friday night.

The International   `25 G8`
23 Wicklow Street, Dublin 2
Phone 677 9250
A pub of two halves offering a nicely preserved Victorian bar downstairs and a popular comedy club upstairs which also acts as a venue for theatre and live bands.

Irish Film Centre   `25 G7`
6 Eustace Street, Temple Bar
Phone 679 5744
Award winning architecture has transformed this Georgian building into a complex which includes two cinemas, a

Neary's on Chatham Street
bookshop, and a bar cum restaurant which are all planned around a glass-covered courtyard.

Kavanagh's   `17 G5`
1 Prospect Square, Glasnevin, Dublin 9
Known as the Gravediggers Arms due to its proximity to Prospect Cemetery, Dublin's main graveyard and the final resting place of many of Ireland's famous sons. The pub has been in the same family since 1833 during which time its traditional roots have been proudly preserved. No TV, no phone, great pint of Guinness.

Kehoe's   `25 G8`
9 South Anne Street, Dublin 2
Phone 6778312
Strange to find a Victorian pub just off Grafton Street which has remained largely unchanged, and where Dubliners still manage to outnumber tourists. Good spot to practise the art of conversation.

Kiely's   `32 J10`
22 Donnybrook Road, Dublin 7
Phone 283 0209
Best known pub in Donnybrook, mainly due to its rugby connections. Leinster's home ground is only a drop kick away, and the players can often be seen here after a match.

Lillie's Bordello   `25 G7`
Adam Court, Grafton Street, Dublin 2
Phone 679 9204
Rather diminutive, but still Dublin's most famous nightclub and pitstop for any A, B or C-lister that sets foot in town. Don't expect to rub shoulders with them, however, as celebrity spotting is hampered by inaccessible VIP areas. Open Monday to Saturday but things

Much unimproved Doheny & Nesbitt!

The Palace Bar on Fleet Street

don't get going until after the pubs shut.

The Long Hall　　　`25 G8`
51 South Great George's St, Dublin 2
Phone 475 1590
Victorian gem which successfully combines the kitsch with the traditional to create a bar which is a real delight. And to cap it all, the staff are friendly and eager to satisfy the thirst of their customers.

The Market Bar　　　`25 G8`
Fade Street, Dublin 2
Phone 613 9094
There is a certain pleasure in finding somewhere that is well hidden. Enter by George's Market or via the courtyard on Fade Street, and discover a former sausage factory that has been transformed into one of the hippest eating and drinking spaces in Dublin. Light cascades from a pitched glass roof, revealing a quirky, minimalist, interior, furnished with park bench style seating. Loud chatter prevails due to the deliberate absence of music, and the excellent tapas serve as an added bonus.

McDaid's　　　`25 G8`
3 Harry Street, Dublin 2
Phone 679 4395
Former city morgue, but more famous for being Brendan Behan's local back in the 1950's. Its location, just off Grafton Street, means that the literati are far outnumbered today by tourists and office workers.

McSorley's　　　`31 H10`
1 Sandford Road, Ranelagh, Dublin 6
Phone497 1595
Looks like a traditional, neighbourhood boozer from outside but inside has a

rather upmarket feel with lots of dark wood, comfortable leather banquettes, and a striking array of sporting photographs. Strong on food, impressive list of wines by the glass, but equally good as a place to enjoy a pint while watching the match.

Messrs Maguire　　　`25 H7`
1-2 Burgh Quay, Dublin 2
Phone 670 5777
Following in the successful footsteps of the Porterhouse, Messrs Maguire brew their own beer on the premises and serve it up in drawing room comfort. Four spacious floors provide lots of table space, and good views of Dublin can be had from a window seat on the top floor.

The Morrison　　　`25 G7`
Ormond Quay, Dublin 1
Phone 887 2400
A rival to the Dylan and nearby Clarence when it comes to trendiest hotel in town, the interiors are the work of Ireland's (and Hong Kong's) most famous designer, John Rocha. The ground floor bars offer plenty of posing space among low tables, comfy leather armchairs and suede sofas. Cool space, cool crowd.

Mulligan's　　　`25 H7`
8 Poolbeg Street, Dublin 2
Phone 677 5582
Mulligan's dates back to 1782 and has changed very little over the years, even retaining its gas lighting. Revered for the fact that it serves, arguably, the best pint of Guinness in Dublin. Former patrons include John F Kennedy who used to drop in while working for Hearst newspapers after World War II. There's no shortage of local characters among today's regulars, and the pub has even been immortalised on film, featuring as the local in *My Left Foot*.

Neary's　　　`25 G8`
1 Chatham Street, Dublin 2
Phone 677 8596
Situated close to the back door of the Gaiety Theatre, it is hardly surprising that Neary's is popular with both the act-

The Pavilion -anyone for cricket?

ing fraternity and their audiences. The pub is easily recognised from outside by a distinctive pair of brass hands, each holding a glass lamp aloft on either side of the entrance. The ornate interior is Edwardian with a busy bar downstairs and a quieter lounge upstairs. A popular spot to quench a thirst brought on by too much retail therapy.

Ocean　　　`26 J8`
Charlotte Quay Dock, Dublin 4
Phone 668 8862
Some things in life are worth seeing, but not worth travelling to see. If you are looking for a waterside setting, and glass fronted, modern architecture, this is for you. Ocean occupies the bottom two floors of an upmarket apartment complex, and serves the rapidly expanding office market which is growing up around it. Therein lies the caveat; as the evening wears on, Dubliners either head home or into town, which can leave the atmosphere a little on the quiet side at times. Good outdoor drinking space when the sun is shining.

Octagon Bar, Clarence Hotel　　　`25 G7`
East Essex Street, Temple Bar
Phone 670 9000
The Clarence Hotel receives endless free publicity by virtue of the fact that it's owned by Bono and the Edge from the rock band, U2. Controversial redevelopment plans drawn up by Norman Foster have recently been given the green light, and would involve temporary closure if they proceed. Time may be running out, therefore, if you want to savour the hotel's wood-panelled Octagon Bar which caters to a mixture of old rockers and a 'freshly shaken dry martini' crowd.

The Odeon　　　`25 G8`
57 Harcourt Street, Dublin 2
Phone 478 2088
What do you do with an old train station? In this case, convert it, very tastefully, into a bar which feels like it ought to be overlooking Barry's tea plantation. It's not quite Raffles Hotel, but there is definitely an air of faded grandeur, with parquet floors and a cool, art deco interior. Ceiling fans seem almost conspicuous by their absence, but art-lined walls, comfy sofas and armchairs all add much to the laid back air. An outdoor terrace provides an ideal spot to sip a cold drink while contemplating just how good life can be as you watch the helter-skelter of the real world outside. Relaxed early on, becoming louder and clubbier as the night draws on. Good spot for Sunday brunch.

O'Donoghue's　　　`25 H8`
15 Merrion Row, Dublin 2

Phone 660 7194
One of Dublin's best known traditional bars, frequented by musicians, most notably members of the Dubliners. Getting to the bar can be a bit of a challenge if you arrive at a busy time (which is virtually all of the time), but Irish enterprise overcomes such adversity with a strategically placed member of staff who stands on the counter so that you can shout your order as you come through the door! A courtyard area outside caters for the overspill. Traditional music sessions every night.

Oliver St John Gogarty   25 G7
58-59 Fleet Street, Dublin 2
Phone 671 1822
First established in 1838, and later named after the famous Irish surgeon, poet, and politician. Wearing his Senator's hat, it was Gogarty who offered the nation economic hope when he suggested that the crossing of a Friesan bull with a queen bee would result in a country flowing with milk and honey. Customers these days, mainly tourists, have to make do with a pint of the amber nectar, although a pint of the dark stuff is a more likely tipple. Live traditional music daily. Musical Pub Crawl starts upstairs at 7.30pm every evening during the summer months (see page 82). Late bar every night of the week.

The Palace   25 G7
21 Fleet Street, Dublin 2
Phone 677 9290
Palace it may be, but a small one which has changed very little over many years. This is a great little pub with a grand wooden bar, tiled floor and attractive leaded glass. Well worth following in the footsteps of the many literary figures who have passed through its doors and now adorn the walls of the back room.

The Pavilion   25 G7
Trinity College, College Green, Dublin 2
Phone 896 1000
The Pav is actually Trinity College's cricket pavilion but on a sunny summer's day it becomes an unrivalled outdoor drinking space, bang in the centre of town, but several lightyears away from the urban grind going on outside of the railings.

POD/Tripod/Crawdaddy/Lobby Bar
Harcourt Street, Dublin 2   25 G8
Phone 476 3374
Constantly evolving, flexible drinking, clubbing and live music space which occupies a set of granite vaults underneath a former railway station. POD (Place of Dance) quickly became Ireland's premier venue for house and garage music when it opened in 1993. It

Dakota on South William Street

has remained ahead of the curve ever since and its latest offering, Tripod, delivers more cutting edge design, the largest dance floor in the city, and a cast of big name DJ's.

The Porterhouse   24 G7
16 Parliament Street, Dublin 2
Phone 679 8847
Fast expanding chain based on a microbrewery concept which has turned them into Ireland's largest Irish-owned brewery. The winning formula is based on a combination of decent pub food, DJ's, live music, and late bar seven nights a week. Sister outlet on Nassau Street.

Pravda   25 G7
35 Liffey St Lower, Dublin 1
Phone 874 0076
It is good to see the north side of the river strike back against the bourgeoisie on the south bank! The truth, or the *pravda*, is that Moscow was never this trendy, with its revolutionary murals, and more varieties of vodka behind the bar than you could shake a stick at. Music is to the fore with a nightly diet of Funk, Soul, House and R & B.

Renards   31 H8
South Frederick Street, Dublin 2
Phone 677 5876
Nightclub that fights it out with Lillie's Bordello in the battle to be the city's top celebrity haunt. Dancefloor downstairs, and VIP area on the first floor, if you feel you warrant it.

Ron Black's   25 H8
37 Dawson Street
Dublin 2
Phone 672 8231
When it comes to upmarket bars and restaurants, Dawson Street is risking an investigation by the Monopolies Commission. The striking interior at Ron Black's is sumptuous, with lots of dark wood panelling and acres of leather. There are three levels, and bags of space for young professional types with deep pockets or a little bit of credit left on their plastic. If you really want to defy the credit crunch, try the Champagne Bar upstairs.

Ryan's   24 E7
28 Parkgate Street, Dublin 8
Phone 677 6097
A fine example of an unspoilt Victorian pub, complete with snugs. Situated near to the entrance of Phoenix Park, regulars argue that Ryan's serves the finest pint in Dublin, a case which is strengthened by the fact that the Guinness Brewery lies just across the river.

Samsara   25 H8
35 Dawson street, Dublin 2
Phone 671 7723
Hard to know what to expect from the outside but worth venturing in to discover one the longest and most attractive bars in town. The decor has Moroccan leanings, while the clientele are high maintenance, cocktail sipping, and determined to see and be seen.

Searson's   31 H9
42-44 Baggot Street Upper, Dublin 4
Phone 660 0330
Large, traditional Irish bar with a modern twist. The reopening of nearby Lansdowne Road stadium will see the return of the special match day atmosphere enjoyed by the local watering holes.

Sin É   25 G7
14-15 Upper Ormond Quay, Dublin 7
Phone 878 7080
Candlelight combined with steep stairs down to the loo give rise to signs such as, 'It's not the fall that kills you but the sudden stop'. If you can manage to find the publicity-shy front door, a good soundtrack, cool crowd, and a laid back atmosphere await within.

JJ Smyth's   25 G8
12 Aungier Street, Dublin 2
Phone 475 2565

Terrace drinkers at the Odeon

The Stag's Head - among the very best of the traditional bars in town

By day, JJ's is a no frills affair, a man's pub. A sign behind the downstairs bar which states that 'women aren't served - you have to bring your own' is not displayed entirely in jest. Worthy of a mention, however, due to its status as something of a night time mecca for jazz and blues enthusiasts. The building was the birth place of the Irish poet, Thomas Moore.

The South William　　`25 G8`
52 South William Street, Dublin 2
Phone 672 5946
Long, narrow bar, modern in style, cool soundtrack, strong on cocktails and, to really make itself stand out from the crowd, an exhaustive list of homemade pies that include some unlikely ingredients, all for €9 a pop.

Spy　　`25 G8`
South William Street, Dublin 2
Phone 677 0014
Intimate cocktail bar and nightclub based in three refurbished Georgian rooms.

The Stag's Head　　`25 G8`
1 Dame Court, Dublin 2
Phone 679 3701
A hidden jewel dating back to the 1870's, the Stag's Head has earned the

rare distinction of featuring on an Irish postage stamp. Little has changed over the years: granite-topped bar, lots of carved mahogany, and eight stained glass windows promoting the stag theme. If you can't get a seat in the main bar, try the back room with its stained glass ceiling or the upstairs lounge. The pub grub is plain, simple and delicious, and includes old favourites such as Irish stew and bacon & cabbage. Downstairs opens at weekends to cope with the extra custom.

Sugar Club　　`25 H8`
8 Lower Leeson Street
Phone 678 7188
Former arts cinema, just off St Stephen's Green. The auditorium feel has been retained, but every second row of banquette seating has been replaced with tables to allow waiter service as you watch live music or comedy on stage. Wood panelled walls, good sound system and a cocktail bar overlooking the serviced area.

The Swan　　`25 G8`
Aungier Street
Phone 475 2722
Feels like a larger version of the Palace - a Victorian bar with lots of carved mahogany and wood paneling. Customers are young and old and include a few medics from the nearby College of Surgeons.

The Temple Bar　　`25 G7`
47/48 Temple Bar, Dublin 2
Phone 672 5287
A 19th century bar that has seen a few changes in recent years. A modern extension successfully combines old with new, offering two pubs for the price of one, linked by 'The Temple Bar Garden'

which is really just a courtyard area where you can catch the afternoon sun while enjoying a ciggy or some pretty decent pub grub. Things get increasingly raucous as the night wears on, and extended opening hours mean that you can grab a late pint and join the throng when many other bars have shut. Irish traditional music on a daily basis.

Thomas Read/The Oak　　`25 G7`
1 Parliament Street, Dublin 2
Phone 671 7283
A little bit of Paris, just across the road from Dublin Castle. Lively café bar, good food and great coffee make Thomas Read's a fashionable spot to while away the day or night. Walk on through to The Oak which has a wood panelled interior stripped from an ocean liner, the Mauretania.

Toner's　　`25 H8`
139 Lower Baggot St, Dublin 2
Phone 676 3090
Not far from St Stephen's Green, Toner's is one of Dublin's most characterful pubs, an authentic spirit grocers which concentrates more on the spirits than the groceries these days. Stone floors add to the rustic feel, and some interesting artefacts help to make it the time capsule that it is.

Traffic　　`25 G7`
54 Middle Abbey St, Dublin 1
Phone 873 4800
Urban chic comes to the north side of the river. Three floors in all, funky soundtrack, young crowd, late night club Thursday to Sunday.

The Vaults　　`25 H7`
Harbourmaster Place, Dublin 1
Phone 605 4700
What used to be ten Victorian brick-built vaults underneath Connolly Station have been cleverly and tastefully transformed into one of the most impressive eating, drinking and clubbing spaces in town.

The Village　　`25 G8`
26 Wexford Street, Dublin 2
Phone 4758555
Formerly Mono and, before that, the Mean Fiddler. Slick and modern bar, club and live music venue.

Whelan's　　`25 G8`
25 Wexford Street, Dublin 2
Phone 478 0766
Large Victorian bar on ground floor but better known as one of the best musical venues in Dublin, staging live performances upstairs every night of the week. Rock, blues, and traditional tastes are all catered for. Lively spot for a late drink even if you're not taking in a band.

---

5 For Style

The Odeon
Ron Black's
Samsara
Café en Seine
Dakota

There are many hundreds of restaurants and cafés to choose from in Dublin, and this guide attempts to select about 80 of the best. This process is bound to be subjective but no apologies are made for that. After all, how many times have you eaten at a restaurant because it happened to be recommended to you by somebody else? All establishments featured have been tried out, often frequently, by somebody connected with the Dublin Street Atlas & Guide. They have been selected by people who enjoy good food and drink, bearing in mind price, location and diversity. These places are the ones that we have enjoyed most - the ones that we recommend to friends and relatives. They don't always agree, and perhaps you won't either, but that's what being subjective is all about! Having said that, we would be keen to hear your own recommendations or any objections that you might have regarding any of our choices.

The restaurant scene in Dublin has been transformed during the Celtic Tiger era. Choice and quality have improved to the extent that Dublin restaurants can now hold their own against most other European capitals. Michelin star establishments include **Chapter One**, **Mint** and **Bon Appétit**, while both **Restaurant Patrick Guilbaud** and **Thornton's** enjoy the rare distinction of a two star rating.

But storm clouds have gathered and Ireland's boom has suddenly given way to recession. A toxic cocktail of credit crunch, falling house and share prices, a strong euro and a series of lousy summers is being served up at the end of an economic shindig that has lasted for a generation. A painful hangover looks sure to follow. Even la creme de la creme will struggle to ride out the economic downturn, while many others will find it difficult to get away with charging € 60 or € 70 per head when their former customers are now looking for a decent nosebag and change out of € 25.

Dubliners are constantly bemoaning the high cost of living in the city - 'rip off Ireland', they call it. We have all had the experience of going somewhere supposedly cheap and cheerful only to find that a couple of drinks and a bottle of plonk end up breaking the bank. On the other hand, there are occasions when it is possible to take advantage of a very reasonable fixed price menu, especially at lunchtime, and leave with both your conscience and the contents of your wallet largely intact! This makes estimating the likely cost of a meal a rather inexact science.

When you add in early bird specials, fixed price menus, and happy hours, attempts to estimate price often tend to

be in vain. The system adopted for this guide, therefore, is rather broad-brush in its approach, attempting to categorise a restaurant as expensive, moderate or cheap.

'Expensive' restaurants are those where you can expect the final bill to exceed € 40 per head. If you eat somewhere categorised as 'cheap', you will, more often than not, escape for less than € 20. The final bill at a restaurant falling into the 'moderate' category should fall somewhere between € 20 and€ 40, bearing in mind all the caveats mentioned earlier.

Finally, the golden rule when using this guide is to phone first! Restaurants come and go at an alarming rate, change ownership, chefs, menus, opening hours and much else, so it's best to check before turning up.

Price Rating

€   **Cheap (usually under € 20 per head)**

€€   **Moderate (usually between € 20 and € 40)**

€€€   **Expensive (€ 40+)**

Phone 832 0690
Price Rating: €€€
Situated at the end of a pier, looking out to sea towards the island of Ireland's Eye, in a building which formerly served as Howth Yacht Club. Cosy bar and a comfortable dining room which is difficult to beat for location, and cooking which manages to live up to the surroundings, with a strong emphasis on fresh seafood. Early bird menu until 7pm. *Opening Times: Tues-Sat12.30pm-3.30pm & 5.30pm-9.30pm; Sun 12noon-5pm & 5.30pm-8.30pm*

Avoca Café   `25 G8`
11-13 Suffolk St, Dublin 2
Phone 672 6019
Price Rating : €
More chatter per square foot than any other dining room in Dublin, as you will hear when you are making your way up to the top floor of this well known craftshop. White walls, red leather banquette seating, a light and airy room, and a sea of ladies lunching. The menu is a straightforward selection of healthy salads, panini and a few bistro staples, followed up by some fab desserts. Before you leave the premises, be sure to check out the deli counter and foodhall in the basement. *Opening Times: Mon-Sat 10am-5.30pm; Sun 11am-5pm*

Aya Food Bar   `25 G8`
49-52 Clarendon St, Dublin 2
Phone 677 1544
Price Rating: €€
Sit at the self-service sushi bar where the dishes pass before you on a conveyor belt, or opt for a table, and select from a menu which is essentially Japanese but with the occasional Irish twist. The 'Sushi 55' option offers all you can eat from the conveyor belt plus a drink for around € 30. If time is scarce, try the food-to-go counter. *Opening Times: Mon-Sun 12.30pm-10pm*

Balzac Brasserie   `25 H8`
35 Dawson Street, Dublin 2
Phone 677 4444
Price Rating: €€€
Parisian styled fine-dining in what used to be the ballroom of a 19th century guildhall. Without doubt, one of the most glamourous and atmospheric dining spaces in town. French cooking to match. *Opening Times: Mon-Fri 12.30pm-2.30pm & 6pm-11pm; Sat 6pm-11pm; sun 5pm-10pm*

Bang Café   `25 H8`
11 Merrion Row, Dublin 2
Phone 676 0898
Price Rating: €€€
Fresh, modern and fashionable - a description which can be applied equally

101 Talbot   `25 H7`   `25 H7`
100-102 Talbot Street, Dublin 1
Phone 874 5011
Price Rating: €€
Conveniently located for the Abbey and Gate Theatres, Talbot Street seems an unlikely place to go looking for good food, but upstairs at number 101 soon changes that view. Bright, simple interior, artwork for sale, and food that is always wholesome and delicious with plenty of choice for vegetarians. Great value pre theatre menu. *Opening Times: Tues-Sat 5pm-11pm*

Alexis Bar & Grill   `41 R13`
17/18 Patrick Street, Dun Laoghaire
Phone 280 8872
Price Rating: €€
Light and modern bistro serving fresh, local, seasonal produce at very keen prices, especially the early bird menu on week days. A rare combination which should guarantee longterm success. *Opening Times: Tues-Fri 12.30pm-2.30pm & 5.30pm-10pm; Sat 5.30pm-10pm; Sun 12.30pm-3pm & 5.50pm-10pm*

Aqua Restaurant   `40 Q12`
1 West Pier, Howth, County Dublin

A delivery of fresh fish arrives at Aqua

to both the decor, the food and, for good measure, to the staff and many of the clientele. An in place since the day it opened almost a decade ago. An outdoor terrace has recently been added for whenever global warming finally hits Dublin. If you are *really* into exclusivity, you could always apply to join **Residence**, a private members club launched by the guys behind Bang, which occupies an elegant 18th century building overlooking St Stephen's Green. *Opening Times: Mon-Sat 12.30pm-3pm & 6pm-11pm*

Bar Italia   `25 G7`
26 Lower Ormond Qy, Dublin 1
Phone 874 1000
Price Rating: €
Part of an expanding family, but remains faithful to the principle of good value, authentic Italian cooking, freshly prepared and served by warm and welcoming Italian staff. *Opening Times: Mon-Sat 10.30am-10.30pm; Sun 1pm-9pm*

Bentley's Oyster Bar & Grill   `25 H8`
22 St Stephen's Green, Dublin 2
Phone 638 3939
Price Rating: €€€
Credit crunch defying transformation of a Georgian townhouse formerly occupied by Brownes Hotel. Irish celebrity chef, Richard Corrigan, has hoovered up a few Michelin stars since leaving these shores to build a culinary empire centred on London's West End but has chosen to launch his latest venture in Dublin. The look is modern and glamourous (the restaurant, not Richard) but it manages to combine seamlessly with the elegance of the Georgian architecture. Fresh seafood naturally dominates the menu but meat eaters are not entirely forgotten. *Opening Times: Mon-Sat 7am-11pm; Sun 7am-*

10pm

Bewley's   `25 H8`
78-79 Grafton St, Dublin 2
Phone 672 7720
Price Rating : €
One minute it shuts up shop after nearly 80 years of trading on this site. Then it makes a quicker return from the dead than Lazarus. Back by popular demand and a 25,000 signature petition, and all the better for the changes made under the new management team from Café Bar Deli. The new layout retains the coffee shop at the front and the in-house theatre on the second floor, with most of the rest given over to the good value Italian fare produced by CBD. Harry Clarke's famous stained glass remains in situ and Grafton Street is no longer missing a front tooth.

Bobo's   `25 G8`
22 Wexford Street, Dublin 2
Phone 400 5750
Price Rating: €
Dublin's traditional chipper has been herded upmarket. Interesting selection of quirky gourmet burgers with an Irish twist (including a few veggie options). Park yourself on the cow hide and feast on the cow - no part of the animal is wasted, which is more than can be said for one or two of the patrons come closing time. *Opening Times: Mon-Fri 9am-11pm; Sat 12noon-11.30pm; Sun 1pm-10pm*

Bodega   `41 R13`
Pavilion Centre
Marine Rd, Dun Laoghaire
Phone 284 2982
Price Rating: €€
Formerly the 40 Foot, the new offering is ultra modern wine bar and tapas. Really comes into its own on a sunny day when

The Winding Stair on Ormond Quay

a table on the outdoor terrace takes in the spectacular sea views over Dublin Bay. No bookings except for parties of 6 or more. *Opening Times: Mon-Sat 12noon-10pm, Sun 12.30pm-9pm*.

Bon Appétit
9 James Terrace, Malahide
Phone 845 0314
Price Rating: €€€+
Despite its slightly peripheral location, Bon Appétit mixes easily with Dublin's biggest culinary beasts. Housed in a handsome Georgian terrace, the signature restaurant occupies two opulent rooms on the first floor, while the ground floor is given over to a comfortable cocktail bar, with a less formal brasserie at basement level. The contemporary French cuisine has earned a Michelin star for the restaurant. Set price menus ease the financial pain, and the brasserie option certainly won't break the bank. *Restaurant is open Tues-Sat 7pm-9.30pm; Friday 12.30-14.30. Brasserie is open Mon-Sat 6pm-10.30pm; Sun 1pm-8pm*

Brasserie Sixty6   `25 G8`
66-67 South Great George's St, Dublin 2
Phone 400 5878.
Price Rating: €€
Deceptively large space serving good value comfort food with a separate menu for veggies. Open daily for breakfast, lunch and dinner. Popular spot for weekend brunch served from 10am to 5pm.

Byblos   `25 G8`
11 St Andrews Street South, Dublin 2
Phone 679 1517
Price Rating: €€
Sister restaurant to the Cedar Tree next door which seems to have been around forever. Authentic Lebanese cuisine, extensive choice including half a dozen mezzes, and belly dancing at weekends. *Opening Times: Mon-Sun 12noon-4.30pm & 5.30pm-11pm*

Café Bar Deli   `25 G8`
13 South Great George's St, Dublin 2
Phone 677 1646
Price Rating: €
Pleasant surroundings that are akin to an old fashioned Parisian café, efficient service and straightforward Mediterranean cuisine which focuses on tasty pasta, pizza and mountainous salads. Not quite as cheap as cooking it yourself, but cheap enough to keep you out of your own kitchen. Usually buzzing. Other outlets in Ranelagh and at Bewley's on Grafton Street. No reservations. *Open: Mon-Sat 12.30pm-11pm; Sun 2pm-10pm*

Carluccio's Caffe   `25 H8`
52 Dawson Street, Dublin 2

Phone 633 3957
Price Rating: €€
If you are looking for the personal touch, it might not be a good idea to eat in a restaurant with a stock market listing, but Carluccio's delivers clean, minimalist style, coupled with modern Italian cooking, and the option of eating alfresco. *Opening Times: Mon-Fri 7am-10.30pm; Sat 8am-10.30pm; Sun 9am-10pm*

Caviston's · 41 S14
59 Glasthule Road, Sandycove
Phone 280 9245
Price Rating: €€
Pine furniture, ceiling fans and mermaid murals may not whet all appetites, but the fish served in this tiny seafood restaurant next door to Caviston's Deli in Sandycove is to die for. Ocean fresh and beautifully cooked. Lunch is served in three ninety minute sittings in order to cope with demand. Menu depends on what was caught earlier that day. A local institution, with a large and loyal following - futile to turn up without a booking. *Opening Times: Tues-Sat 12noon-5pm*

Chapter One · 17 G8
18 Parnell Square, Dublin 1
Phone 873 2266
Price Rating: €€€
Generally considered to be Dublin's finest restaurant north of the river. Situated below Dublin Writers Museum, the decor incorporates the original stone walls but manages to achieve a warm and comfortable ambience, equally conducive to business or pleasure. The service is friendly and seamless, the long held reputation for *haute cuisine* is well deserved, and the wine list is one of the finest in town. With its proximity to the Gate and the Abbey, it is a popular choice for theatre-goers, some of whom come early for a starter and main course, and return after the show for dessert. If your budget doesn't stretch to fine dining, try lunch at the **Chapterhouse Cafe** upstairs in the Writers Museum. *Opening Times: Tues-Fri 12.30pm-2.30pm & 6pm-11pm; Sat 6pm-11pm.*

Cornucopia · 25 G8
19 Wicklow Street, Dublin 2
Phone 677 7583
Price Rating: €
For more than 20 years, this popular vegetarian restaurant has been serving a wide selection of imaginative dishes at very reasonable prices. *Opening Times: Mon-Sat 8.30am-8pm (until 9pm Thurs); Sun 12noon-7pm*

Diep Le Shaker · 32 J9
55 Pembroke Lane, Dublin 2
Phone 661 1829
Price Rating: €€€
Upmarket Thai restaurant, serving traditional classics with a modern twist. Generally considered to serve the best Thai food in town. A cheaper and less formal option available at **Diep Noodle Bar** in Ranelagh. *Opening Times: Mon-Fri: 12noon-2.30pm (until 5pm Fri) & 5pm-10.30pm, Sat: 6pm-11.30pm*

Dunne & Crescenzi · 25 H8
South Frederick Street, Dublin 2
Phone 677 3815
Price Rating: €
For some, Italy is all about Prada, Gucci, and D&G. D&C, on the other hand, specialise in bringing authentic *enoteca* atmosphere to Dublin. Their burgeoning empire is based on rustic good looks, deli style food, and heart warming wine by the glass or bottle. Has spawned a few imitators but D&C remains top of the pile. *Open: Mon-Sat 7.30am-11pm, Sun 10pm-10pm*

Eden · 25 G7
Meeting House Square, Temple Bar
Phone 670 5372
Price Rating: €€€
The contemporary design exudes self-confidence, and the outdoor terrace overlooking the square is good for a spot of alfresco dining on a summer's day. Not as 'in' a place as it once was perhaps, but consistently high standards of modern Irish cooking and service help to ensure that its premier league status is retained. *Opening Times: Mon-Sun 12.30pm-3pm & 6pm-10.30pm*

Elephant & Castle · 25 G7
18 Temple Bar, Dublin 2
Phone 679 3121
Price Rating : €€
American style cooking served up in simple, informal surroundings by friendly staff. Busy the whole day long. The house speciality is the elephantburger, but alternatives include an exhaustive selection of omelettes, and some excellent salads and pasta dishes. The legendary spicy chicken wings seem designed to satisfy the appetite of a Texan oilman - so, it might be a good idea to share. Reservations are not accepted, but you can put your name on

Caviston's - more than 50 years in Sandycove

a waiting list if there are no tables free, and pop over the road for a drink while you're waiting. *Open: Mon-Fri 8am-11.30pm, Sat & Sun 10.30am-11.30pm*

Ely CHQ · 25 H7
Customs House Quay, Dublin 1
Phone 672 0010
Price Rating : €€
Another *Sex And The City* location from Ely, who are proven masters at the wine bar cum bistro combo. The winning formula is wines from around the globe, more than 90 by the glass, meat sourced from their own organic farm in county Clare, efficient but friendly service and stylish surroundings. At CHQ, it's Bollinger umbrellas, big outdoor terrace, waterside location amid the high rise financial quarter and a clientele which mixes suits with tables of yummy mummies meeting for a bit of ladies who lunch. Credit crunch, what credit crunch? *Opening Times: Mon-Fri 8am-11.30pm, Sat 1pm-12.30am*

Ely HQ · 26 J7
Hanover Quay, Dublin 2
Phone 633 9986
Price Rating : €€
See above. The HQ in this instance stands for Hanover Quay, an area which resembles a mini version of London's Canary Wharf. Lunch and after work are the best times if you are looking for a lively atmosphere. Slightly out of town, but will benefit from the completion of the landmark Grand Canal Square, the Luas extension on other side of the river and the new Samuel Beckett Bridge. The vast interior is cleverly divided in order to retain a degree of intimacy. Staff, like the wine, are from the four corners of globe. Modern cooking, with a strong emphasis on fish dishes, delivers a tasty

---

5 For Business

L'Ecrivain
Thornton's
Patrick Guilbaud
Shanahan's
Chapter One

Fallon & Byrne on Exchequer Street

plate of food and a glass of wine for € 30. If Richard Rogers designed a wine bar, it would probably look something like this. *Opening Times: Mon-Fri 12noon-3pm & 5.30pm-10pm, Sat 1pm-5.30pm*

Ely Wine Bar `25 H8`
22 Ely Place, Dublin 2
Phone 676 8986
Price Rating: €€
The original (see two entries above). If you are after a single plate of something to satisfy your taste buds, and a glass or two of your favourite tipple to wash it down, then this is the place for you. It occupies the ground floor of a Georgian townhouse, plus a recently extended and more convivial basement area. The wine list is extensive and the staff are knowledgeable and only too happy to share their opinions with you. *Open: Mon-Sat 12noon-12midnight*

Enoteca delle Langhe `25 G7`
Quartiere Bloom, Lower Ormond Qy
Phone 888 0834
Price Rating: €
Part of a development on the north side of the Millennium Bridge which has become Dublin's little Italy. Take a seat indoors or out, and enjoy a glass of soothing red wine and a platter of cured ham, salami and cheese. A little slice of the *la dolce vita*, without having to carry out the Italian Job to pay for it.

Fallon & Byrne `25 G8`
11-17 Exchequer Street, Dublin 2
Phone 472 100
Price Rating: €€
New York meets Paris meets Dublin. Industrial size unit which effortlessly combines a food emporium, juice bar, café, brasserie and wine bar. A place

where you can easily be parted from your cash, but it is possible to enjoy the ab fab surroundings while nursing a coffee and a snack and still get change out of € 10. *Opening Times for Food Hall: Mon-Fri: 8am-10pm, Sat 9am-9pm, Sun 11am-9pm*

The French Paradox `26 J8`
53 Shelbourne Road, Dublin 4
Phone 660 4068
Price Rating: €€
Ballsbridge is home to an increasing number of trendy delis which cater to the sort of palate which can distinguish between virgin and extra virgin olive oil. The French Paradox is tiny, upstairs and down, but manages to achieve a combination of wine shop, wine bar, deli and diner. It is an absolute treat to secure a table, and share a couple of their Mediterranean style platters of Spanish hams, Italian antipasti, cured fish, foies gras and cheeses, all complemented by a superb choice of wines by the glass. A place that delights in the quality of their food, wine, service, and general ambience. *Food is served: Mon-Fri from 12noon-3pm & 6pm-10.30pm, Sat 12noon-10.30pm*

Fresh `25 G8`
Powerscourt Townhouse, Clarendon St
Dublin 2
Phone 671 9669
Price Rating: €
If your body is a temple and your pockets are not as deep as they might be, take advantage of a wholesome range of soups, sandwiches, veggie meals, herbal teas and juices that come with a good view of the masses below and very little financial pain. *Opening Times: Mon-Sat 10am-6pm (until 7pm on Thursdays)*

Gotham Café `25 G8`
8 South Anne Street, Dublin 2
Phone 679 5266
Price Rating: €
New York theme café which is always buzzing, partly due to it's location just off Grafton Street, but mainly because its customers keep coming back to sample the gourmet pizzas, interesting pastas and salads, and the warm and friendly atmosphere. *Opening Times: Mon-Sun*

12noon-11pm

Govinda's `25 G8`
4 Aungier Street, Dublin 2
Phone 475 0309
Price Rating: €
Extremely cheap vegetarian restaurant run by Hare Krishna. No pressure to sign up for a haircut and Tibetan robes though, so go ahead and enjoy excellent value curries, kebabs and burgers. No booze. Other branches on Merrion Row and Middle Abbey Street. *Opening Times: Mon-Sat 12noon-9pm*

Gruel `25 G7`
68a Dame Street, Dublin 2
Phone 670 7119
Price Rating: €
The interior is more Steptoe's yard than Philippe Starke, but delightfully unpretentious. The menu is also a little eccentric - a different 'roast in a roll' for each day of the week but, once again, it scores highly. Supper menu from the blackboard after 5pm includes delicious pastas, fishcakes, bangers & mash and a good selection of veggie options. An eclectic soundtrack completes an inexpensive and altogether enjoyable experience. *Opening Times: Mon-Sun 12noon-10pm*

Harvey Nichols `37 J14`
Dundrum Town Centre, Dublin 16
Phone 291 0488
Price Rating: €€€
Ground floor café and first floor restaurant and bar, both housed in a post modern, glass box structure which can be accessed through the store. As one might expect, the decor is bold but sophisticated, and the food and service live up to the high standards associated with the Harvey Nick's brand. *Restaurant Opening Times: Mon 12.30-3pm, Tues-Sat 12.30pm-3pm & 6pm-10pm, Sun 12.30pm-4pm*

IFSC `25 H7`
Here beats the palpitating heart of the Celtic Tiger. Dublin's International Financial Services Centre has been the catalyst for the regeneration of a huge swathe of the city's run down river front and, where office blocks have risen, there are hungry workers to feed. If you have an hour or two to spare for lunch, and enjoy the fact that your fellow diners are all toiling hard at the coal face, head for Mayor Square and familiarise yourself with the new face of Dublin. The culinary highlights include **eno winebar** (above their excellent wine shop) **Lagoona Bar, Il Fornaio**, as well as an array of more familiar names such as **Bar Italia, Milano**, and **La Corte**.

---

5 On The Cheap

Café Bar Deli
Steps of Rome
Lemon Crepe
Govinda's
Gruel

Il Baccaro `25 G7`
Meeting House Square, Dublin 2
Phone 671 4597
Price Rating: €€
Meeting House Square is a stark, new piazza, but Il Baccaro conjures up images of a medieval drinking vault in the bowels of Prague. Fun place, with good humoured Italian staff on hand to keep the warm house red flowing by the carafe. The food is plain and simple, the prices are affordable and, if you prefer life above ground, there are a few tables outside in the summer. *Opening Times: Mon-Fri 6pm-11pm, Sat 12noon-3pm & 6pm-11pm, Sun 6pm-11pm*

Imperial Chinese `25 G8`
12a Wicklow Street, Dublin 2
Phone 677 2580
Price Rating: €€
Enjoyable Cantonese cuisine every day of the week, but Sunday tends to be when members of the Chinese community arrive in force to partake of the legendary dim sum. *Opening Times: Mon-Sun 12noon-11.30pm*

Independent Pizza Company `17 H5`
28 Lower Drumcondra Rd, Dublin 9
Phone 830 2044
Price Rating: €
Busy, friendly, local pizzeria which has been serving some of the tastiest pizzas in town since 1984. *Opening daily 12noon-11pm*

Itsa4 `33 K9`
6a Sandymount Green, Dublin 4
Phone 219 4676
Price Rating: €€
If you are visiting Dublin for the weekend, it's unlikely that you'll stray this far from the city centre, but if you want to sample quintessential middle class life in the city's southern suburbs, hop on the DART, head to Sandymount, and get yourself to this posh diner overlooking the village green. The clientele is mainly local with a healthy sprinkling of yummie mummies. Cap it off with a bracing walk along Sandymount Strand before heading back to inner city reality. *Opening Times: Tues-Sat 12noon-3pm & 5.30pm-10pm; Sun 12noon-8pm*

Jaipur `25 G8`
41 South Great George's St, Dublin 2
Phone 677 0999
Price Rating: €€
No flock wallpaper here. Light and modern setting matched by a contemporary approach to Indian cooking. *Opening Times: Mon-Sun 5.30-11pm*

Kilkenny Restaurant & Café `25 H8`
6 Nassau Street, Dublin 2
Phone 677 7066

Ely CHQ on Customs House Quay

Price Range : €
Situated on the first floor of the Kilkenny Shop, famous for its range of Irish clothing and craft goods, the dining area is modern and spacious. A good range of wholesome lunches are on offer, backed up by an interesting variety of home baked breads, cakes and biscuits which you can buy to eat in or take away. Join an endless stream of hungry shoppers and office workers, and try to get a table by the window where you can gaze into the more peaceful world of Trinity College. *Open: Mon-Sat 8.30am-5.30pm (until 7pm on Thurs), Sun 11am-5pm*

La Cave `25 G8`
28 South Anne street, Dublin 2
Phone 679 4409
Price Rating: €€
There is something about basement premises that discourage idle inquiry. La Cave has been here for 20 year and most Dubliners will have walked past its front door hundreds of times without once satisfying their curiosity. What they are missing is a tiny, quintessentially French winebar, with a few seats at the bar and half a dozen tables. Where Ely is hip and modern, the decor here belongs to another age, but that's not necessarily a bad thing when combined with service that is personal and informative, and food which is nicely cooked and relatively inexpensive. Look out for the organised wine tastings. *Open Mon-Sat 12.30pm until late, Sun 6pm until late*

La Corte `25 G8`
Powerscourt Townhouse, Clarendon St
Phone 633 4477
Price Rating: €
Arrive early for lunch at this popular

Italian café to secure a table with a bird's eye view of the goings-on below.

La Maison des Gourmets `25 G8`
15 Castle Market, off Drury St, Dublin 2
Phone 672 7258
Price Rating: €
Ground floor boulangerie where the smell of freshly baked bread fills the air, and small first floor café where you can sample the produce not long after it has left the oven. Soups, warm open sandwiches, salads and a selection of cured meats. Vive la France! *Opening Times: Mon-Sat 8am-7pm, Sun 11am-5pm.*

L'Ecrivain `25 H8`
109a Lower Baggot Street, Dublin 2
Phone 661 1919
Price Rating: €€€+
Some restaurants serve great food but

Delicious patisserie at Léon

Peploe's - Dublin's answer to the Ivy

lack atmosphere while others are let down by erratic service. L'Ecrivain, however, excels on all fronts. There is always a buzz, a lot of suits at lunchtime, but an interesting mix of business and pleasure is generally the order of the day. They come for modern Irish cooking at its best, generous portions, and service which is not too formal, just spot on. Certainly not cheap, but brilliant overall. *Open: Mon-Fri 12.30pm-2pm & 7pm-11pm; Sat 7pm-11pm*

Lemon Crepe & Coffee Co   `25 G8`
66 South William Street, Dublin 2
Phone 672 9044
Price Rating: €
Tiny pancake joint, easily identified by the lunchtime queue for its cheap and delicious sweet and savoury crepes. Seats inside and out. Order and pay at the till before you sit. Smarter looking outlet on Dawson Street.

Léon Bistro   `25 G8`
33 Exchequer Street, Dublin 2
Phone 670 7238
Price Rating: €€
A little slice of Paris right in the heart of Dublin. The dining room is modest in size but makes up for it with a rather grand gilt mirror and a theatrical chandelier. Good bistro food is trumped by irresistible patisserie. Two nearby Léon Cafés on Wicklow Street and Trinity Street (marked by the lunchtime queues out of the door) with further expansion plans in the pipeline.

L'Gueuleton   `25 G8`
1 Fade Street
Phone 675 3708
Price Rating: €€
Caused quite a few ripples of excitement

when it opened a few years back for offering authentic, rustic French cooking at affordable prices. At 6pm there is still a queue outside door to secure a reservation for later the same evening, but the prices have crept upwards and the food can occasionally be hit and miss. *Opening Times: Mon-Sat 12.30pm-3pm & 6pm-10pm*

Lock's   `31 G9`
1 Windsor Terrace, Dublin 8
Phone 454 3391
Price Rating: €€€
Quiet location, overlooking the Grand Canal in Portobello. Combine drawing room comfort with refined bistro cooking which takes advantage of the best, locally sourced, seasonal ingredients and it's bound to come at a price. But you do get what you pay for. *Opening Times: Mon-Sat 12noon-3pm & 6pm-10.30pm; Sun 12.30pm-4pm*

Mermaid Café   `25 G7`
69/70 Dame St, Dublin 2
Phone 670 8236
Price Rating: €€€
Smallish restaurant with a decor which looks like it was inspired by New England Shakers and a menu which is not without some American influence as well. Mouth watering food is complemented by a fine wine list and very personable service. Always busy, and the decibel level can be very high at times. Top place for Sunday brunch. *Open: Mon-Sat 12.30pm-2.30pm & 6pm-11pm; Sun 12.30pm-3pm & 6pm-9pm*

Milano   `25 G8`
38 Dawson Street, Dublin 2
Phone 670 7744
Price Rating: €€
British chain, Pizza Express, prefer to operate in Ireland under the assumed name of Milano. What you get, however, is very much as you would expect - well chosen locations, designer interiors, pleasant service, a smart young crowd, and pizzas that are as good as you'll find anywhere in Dublin. Other city centre outlets on East Essex Street and Excise Walk. *Opening Times: Mon-Sat 12noon-12midnight, Sun 12noon-11pm*

5 For Wooing

Bentley's
Venu
Peploe's
Balzac
Town Bar & Grill

Mint   `31 H10`
47 Ranelagh Village, Dublin 6
Phone 497 8655
Price Rating: €€€+
Ranelagh Village is now only a few minutes by Luas from the centre of town. Don't be put off by the underwhelming exterior. Inside is tasteful and patrolled by a legion of black suited striplings. The atmosphere is similar to Thorntons - the reverence shown towards the Michelin star food does not exactly contribute to a fun atmosphere. But the cooking is nothing short of spectacular (foam is almost guaranteed) and reasonably priced, but it is difficult to avoid a financial battering when there is no wine by the glass, house wine, and the winelist is short on bottles costing less than € 100. *Opening Times: Tues-Wed 6.30pm-10.30pm, Thurs-Fri 12.30pm-2.30pm & 6.30pm-10.30pm, Sat 6.30pm-10.30pm*

Nonna Valentina   `31 G9`
1-2 Portabello Road
Dublin 8
Phone 454 9866
Price Rating: €€
Part of the expanding Dunne & Crescenzi empire, and named after the owner's grandmother. Housed in modest but nicely appointed premises overlooking the Grand Canal, the service and cooking are equally precise with classic Italian cuisine the order of the day. *Opening Times: Mon-Sun 12noon-11pm*

One Pico   `25 H8`
5-6 Molesworth Place, Dublin 2
Phone 676 0300
Price Rating: €€€
Premier league food and impeccable service in an intimate setting (the waiters have to pass single file between tables). A place to celebrate birthdays, anniversaries, or just the joy of eating. Best not to bring the mistress though, as this is the realm of politicians, journalists and businessmen who enjoy conspicuous consumption. Excellent wine list to complement fine Irish cooking, and a cheese board to die for. *Opening Times: Mon-Sat 12.30pm-2.30pm & 6pm-11pm*

Parnell Street   `25 G6`
Not a restaurant, but a rather run down street, north of the river, which is showing embryonic signs of becoming Dublin's Chinatown. Some smart frontages are beginning to appear, and the mix of Chinese, Korean and Thai cuisine on offer tends to be cheaper and more authentic than much of what is available fifteen minutes walk away in the centre of town.

Peploes Wine Bistro   `25 G8`
16 St Stephen's Green, Dublin 2

Phone 676 3144
Price Rating: €€€
Occupies the basement of a beautiful, ivy-clad, Georgian terrace. The room is divided between a bar and informal seating area, and a restaurant space which is dominated by a huge mural depicting celebrity diners, ranging from Bill Clinton and Nelson Mandela to Luciano Pavarotti (some night that must have been). Often described as Dublin's answer to the Ivy, space is somewhat more limited, as is the celebrity quotient, but the food does concentrate on uncomplicated bistro classics. Great location for a power lunch, and equally good for a social whirl. Wine list is extensive, and includes a few bottles marked 'price on demand' (surely if you have to ask, you are unlikely to afford). One of the hottest tables in town. *Open daily 12noon-11pm*

Port House   `25 G8`
64a South William Street, Dublin 2
Phone 677 0298
Price Rating: €€
The only restaurant guaranteed to carry on when the lights have gone out every where else in Dublin. An ocean of candles light this stone vaulted space which adds an air of romance (although it might be helpful to offer the menu in braille). The Porterhouse are behind this venture which attempts to bring us the first decent tapas bar in Dublin. This is a good effort and the response has been encouraging enough for them to open a sister establishment, **Bar Pintxo**, on Eustace Street in Temple Bar. Fun place.

Queen of Tarts   `25 G7`
4 Cork Hill, Dame St, Dublin 2
Phone 670 7499
Price Rating: €
Small tea room which produces some wonderful, and cheap, home baking. If you can't get in, try their new place around the corner on Cow's Lane which is bigger and even boasts an outdoor terrace. *Opening Times: Mon-Fri 7.30am-7pm; Sat & Sun 8.30am-7pm*

Rasam   `41 S14`
18-19 Glasthule Road, Dun Laoghaire
Phone 230 0600
Price Rating: €€
Situated above the Eagle pub, this is Indian food served in a very classy setting that is worth going a little bit out of your way for. The menu gives a brief but helpful description of each dish and where it comes from. *Open daily 5pm-11pm*

Restaurant Patrick Guilbaud   `25 H8`
21 Upper Merrion Street, Dublin 2
Phone 676 4192
Price Rating : €€€+

Nonna Valentina by the Grand Canal

This is the prize heavyweight (or coq of the walk) of Dublin's French restaurants. The food takes advantage of a ready supply of fresh Irish ingredients, but the cooking is rigorously French and qualifies for a mention in all of the good food guides (Guilbaud's was the first restaurant in Ireland to be awarded two Michelin stars). Such a pedigree, however, comes at a price. Although there are some reasonably priced set menus, this is the land of expense account dining - so, if you intend paying by cash, be careful not to fall off your wallet when you sit down. *Opening Times: Tues-Sat 12.30pm-2pm & 7.30pm-10.15pm*

RhodesD7   `25 G7`
Mary's Abbey, Dublin 7
Phone 804 4444
Price Rating: €€€
British celebrity chefs seem able to get away with operating an armful of outlets despite having only one pair of hands. In bringing his particular brand to Dublin, Gary Rhodes has chosen a rather unfashionable part of town, albeit a handy one for the legal profession who are well known for keeping their snouts in the trough. As one would expect, both the food and the service are well delivered, but the jury is still out regarding location. *Opening Times: Tues-Sat 12noon-10pm*

Riva   `26 J7`
Hanover Quay
Dublin 2
Phone 675 3577
Price Rating: €€
It's a sunny day (use your imagination) and your idea of dining alfresco does not involve inhaling exhaust fumes. Riva may be the answer. Wine bar cum bistro with lots of outdoor seating and an attractive waterside location in one of Dublin's burgeoning dockside developments.

Roly's Bistro   `32 J9`
7 Ballsbridge Terrace, Dublin 4
Phone 668 2611
Price Rating: €€€
When it opened back in 1992, Roly's

quickly became one of the most popular places in town. The fact that it has remained so owes much to the high standards of cooking and service, as well as a fashionable location close to the American embassy and RDS. The menu may change but the food is always nicely prepared, keenly priced, and served up in a very relaxed atmosphere. *Opening Times: Mon-Sun 12-3pm & 6pm-10pm*

Saba   `25 G8`
26-28 Clarendon Street, Dublin 2
Phone 679 2000
Price Rating: €€
Authentic Thai and Vietnamese cooking dished up in a refreshingly contemporary space that used to be home to the Rajdoot. If you are looking for pedigree, you'll be pleased to know that the head chef has cooked for the King and Queen of Thailand. *Open daily 12noon until late*

Shanahans on the Green   `25 G8`
119 St Stephen's Green, Dublin 2
Phone 407 0939
Price Rating: €€€+
If you hail from Texas and find it difficult to comprehend how an eight ounce morsel of steak could possibly constitute a full meal, then you have landed on your feet here. Georgian elegance meets American style steakhouse, serving anything up to 24 ounces of Irish Angus beef, although there are plenty of alternatives to steak if you are not into red meat. Celebrity haunt. *Opening Times: Mon-Sun 6pm-10.30pm. Also open for lunch Friday and Sunday*

The Saddle Room   `25 H8`
27 St Stephen's Green, Dublin 2
Phone 663 4500
Price Rating: €€€

Mermaid Cafe on Dame Street

Lunch at the Powerscourt Townhouse

The Shelbourne Hotel has made a welcome return after a squillion euro refurb that, to their credit, has not detracted from the original Georgian grandeur. The Saddle Room is built for comfort, like a few of its patrons, but there's an eclectic mix of wealthy American hotel guests and business class Dubliners. Both the food and the service are slightly old school, but very well delivered.

Silk Road Cafe `25 G8`
Chester Beatty Library
Dublin Castle, Dublin 2
Phone 407 0770
Price Rating: €
The Chester Beatty Library (see page 74) is one of Dublin's hidden gems, and the same can be said for its cafe which serves delicious Middle Eastern food, much of it vegetarian, all of it halal and kosher. *Opening Times: Tues-Fri 10am-4.30pm; Sat 11am-4.30pm; Sunday 1pm-4.30pm*

Simon's Place Coffee Shop `25 G8`
22 South Great Georges St, Dublin 2
Phone 679 7821
Price Rating: €
In keeping with the neighbouring St Georges Arcade, the vibe is hippy chic meets backpacker. Heart warming soup, freshly made doorstep sandwiches, panini and wraps, salads and a good selection of home-baked cakes and buns. Cheap but satisfying. *Opening Times: Mon-Sun 8am-7pm*

Steps of Rome `25 G8`
1 Chatham Street, Dublin 2
Phone 670 5630
Price Rating: €
Small, one roomed diner staffed by Italians who know a thing or two about how to make a proper espresso, delicious

pasta, and scrumptious pizza which comes by the slice. Seats are at a premium but prices are bargain basement. *Opening Times: Mon-Sun 10am-12midnight*

Thornton's `25 G8`
128 St Stephen's Green, Dublin 2
Phone 478 7008
Price Rating: €€€+
Thornton's occupies the first floor of the Fitzwilliam Hotel. A recent refurb has employed a warmer colour palette and added a Canape Bar to the layout. Kevin Thornton's cooking has received many accolades, and the restaurant holds two Michelin stars. The combination of French *haute cuisine* and a seamlessly run operation does not come cheap, but many people will go far out of their way to eat here. Perhaps that is its only weakness - the reverence shown towards the food can sometimes contribute to a slightly rarefied atmosphere. *Open: Tues-Sat 12.30pm-2pm & 7pm-9.30pm*

Town Bar & Grill `25 H8`
21 Kildare Street
Dublin 2
Phone 662 4742
Price Rating: €€€
Located in the cellars of Mitchell's Wine Merchants, the interior is urban chic, the cooking is modern Italian, and the clientele are a mix of local suits and socialites. *Opening Times: Mon-Sun 12.30-11pm*

Tribeca `31 H10`
65 Ranelagh
Phone 497 4174
Price Rating: €€
New York style, neighbourhood eatery, with lots of stalwarts on the menu, including chicken wings and burgers, but plenty of interesting alternatives and an ever changing specials board. Busy, busy, busy, but reservations only accepted on the day. *Opening Times: Mon-Sun 12noon-11pm*

Uki Yo `25 G8`
7-9 Exchequer Street, Dublin 2
Phone 633 4071
Price Rating: €€

Lock's on the Grand Canal

Sake bar serving Japanese and Korean cuisine. If the food sometimes lacks authenticity, the fun atmosphere makes up for it, especially if you commandeer one of the karaoke booths downstairs. *Opening Times: Mon-Sat 12noon-4pm & 5pm-11pm, Sun 5pm-11pm*

Venu `25 G8`   `25 G8`
Anne's Lane
Dublin 2
Phone 670 6755
Price Rating: €€€
You never know what to expect from basement premises and, from the outside, it doesn't look terribly inspiring. Inside, however, the decor is uber cool and contemporary. There are family connections to Restaurant Patrick Guilbaud, the daddy of fine dining in Ireland. No surprise then that the cooking is classic European and everything runs like clockwork. Great cocktail bar. *Opening Times: Tues-Sun 12.30pm-3pm & 6pm-11pm*

Wagamama `25 G8`
South King Street, Dublin 2
Phone 478 2152
Price Rating: €
Part of a chain of Japanese noodle bars which base their success on a designer cool, minimalist, interior where diners sit at long communal bench tables and choose from an excellent range of keenly priced rice and noodle dishes. *Opening Times: Mon-Sat 12noon-11pm; Sun 12noon-10pm*

The Winding Stair `25 G7`
40 Lower Ormond Quay
Dublin 1
Phone 872 7320
Price Rating: €€€
The name is synonymous with the bookshop below, which closed in 2005 but was reborn a year later. The restaurant enjoys views over the Ha'penny Bridge and specialises in simple, high quality Irish cooking using mainly organic ingredients. Extensive wine list. *Opening Times: Mon-Sun 12.30pm-3.30pm & 6pm-10.30pm (until 9.30pm Sun)*

Yamamori `25 G8`
71-72 South Great George's St
Dublin 2
Phone 475 5001
Price Rating : €€
Yamamori is a fun place to eat at relatively low prices. The portions are generous and the Japanese cooking is full of flavour. Noodles are the speciality of the house, but there are also plenty of sushi, tempura, and chargrilled meat and fish options. Good choice for vegetarians. Second outlet on Lower Ormond Quay. *Opening Times: Mon-Sun 12.30pm-11pm*